24/7 French Lessons

My Quest to Learn French in a Dordogne Village

Written and Photography by

Karen Eberwein

Coastside Press

Half Moon Bay, California

ISBN 978-0-692-46191-4

To Steve, Rachel, Jill and
the wonderful people of Cénac & Domme

Note to Reader: All conversations are in French
except when noted

Introduction

My high school French class was torture. Conjugating verbs and rote memorization numbed my brain. Plus my French teacher spoke in English most of the time, except when she was telling us to *"Fermez la bouche,"* which means "Shut up." It's a miracle that through all the drudgery and unimaginative classes, I retained my love of the French language and culture. Growing up in a small agricultural town of 3,000 in Central California was a long way from France or anything remotely French. Laughing Cow cheese did not count, even though it was often found in my refrigerator. As a teenager in 1978, I found a way to travel by being an American Field Service exchange student. For a year I lived in New Zealand, an amazing country, with an even more amazing family. However, the only foreign language I learned was the Queen's English.

French was always the language I most desired to learn, but I could never figure out a way to live in France for a significant length of time. I knew a total immersion experience would be the best classroom for me. Fast forward through university, working in San Francisco, a happy marriage, raising two wonderful daughters, and retiring young to a window of opportunity to have another quasi-AFS year. My parents and daughters were healthy and independent. It was time for the adventure of a lifetime. It was time to learn French in France.

With a French dictionary, a camera, and a full heart, my husband and I landed in the Dordogne Valley one cold December 1st. My plan was to spend almost a year in the Dordogne for a period of intensive study. My husband would come and go back to the United States. For me, everyday life would be my classroom, and strangers would be my teachers. My motto was "No French conversation is too short; no French person is unable to teach me something; and no situation is too difficult not to speak French." Granted, it was a long motto, so it won't be stitched on a pillow. Often the need to survive facilitates the ability to learn, thus my philosophy – "jump in for a total immersion" - was born.

I remember reading Frances Mayes' *Under The Tuscan Sun,* and it seemed like the main character made strong friendships immediately after she arrived. I thought, How did she do that? That can't be real. Another book, *Round Ireland With A Fridge* written by Tony Hawk, included his escapades not only with a fridge, but also with loads of friends he made in the villages along the route he walked. Making friends seemed effortless for him. Even in *Eat, Pray, Love,* Elizabeth Gilbert made meaningful connections in her adopted foreign homes, and I wondered, is that possible? Now, since I have been so extremely lucky to spend almost a year in the Dordogne Valley, I am able to answer those questions. It was possible, but it was not a reward based on time spent. There was no formula for number of days in village equals percentage of residents accepting you. Maybe the answer to why I went beyond the typical tourist experience was due to the fact that I loved being in France and it showed. I was in awe of this place and the people. The customs, along with the beauty of the language, agreed with me and brought out a different side

of me. For most of this trip, I didn't recognize myself. I was open, trusting, and friendly with strangers. How else could I learn a language if not by talking and listening to people? In pursuit of new vocabulary and mastery of new verb tenses, I received a wonderful added benefit time and time again: new friendships. Friendships grew faster than my French. That was the definition of a win/win situation: a friend who spoke French. It helped that I was able to laugh at myself and that I wasn't afraid to make mistakes. I did both regularly and often, starting the very first evening of our arrival.

Je m'appelle Karen

(My name is Karen)

By the time we landed at the Bordeaux airport and drove for three hours east to Cénac et St. Julien, it was dark. Millions of stars were out, along with several spotlights on featured historic buildings and castles. We found our little stone house with dark brown, shuttered windows perched on the hillside above the downtown of the village. The front door was unlocked, so we entered into the sunroom. There on the side table, the house keys waited for us. They looked like large, iron pirate keys. Already I liked this community, just for the fact that it was safe to leave a house unlocked. Even though it was night, we knew the wicker bench opposite the south facing large windows would be an ideal spot to enjoy the morning sunshine and the view of the hills. Another door led us into a large, open room that was the sitting room, dining room, and kitchen. Three windows spaced along the downhill side of the house offered more views of the hills and the slate tiles of the rooftops.

The furniture was positioned close to the all-important wood-burning stove and the television. There was a bedroom with fireplace off of the sitting room. The dark wooden beams along the ceiling and two-foot-thick stone walls were pleasing, but the most charming feature of the first floor was the narrow, wooden, completely crooked staircase tucked in the corner. If I stood on a step with my feet wide apart, one foot would be higher than the other, even though I was on the same step, that's how wonderfully crooked it was. Upstairs there were two bedrooms, a long hallway with closets, and a bathroom. No matter how tall you were, it was necessary to duck your head when entering the bathroom, or else you would hit the wooden beams due to the steep pitch of the roof. One extremely small triangular dormer window with decorative wood design let light in above the bathtub. As I carefully walked back downstairs, I recalled from the rental paperwork that the house should have a second bathroom, but where was it? In my excitement to enter my new French home, it turns out that I overlooked another door right beside a second front door in the sunroom. The British term "water closet" gives a true, realistic description of our downstairs bathroom. Somehow, a toilet, sink, and coffin-like shower fit in that little space. Lack of room was not the worst characteristic of the bathroom though; it was the lack of heat that made a wintertime trip to the loo a dreaded experience.

As we unpacked and explored the rooms, delighting in their character and charm, there was a knock at the door. Ready or not, my French education was about to start. My next-door neighbor, who acted as the house manager of my vacation home, stood on my doorstep with a big smile. "Hello, Karen. You have arrived. I saw the lights in the house, and I had to come by to say hello," she said in French. Claire spoke rapid French. She was a small person, but her energy filled the room. Her short blonde hair and her hands moved as she talked. Her eyes sparkled behind her chunky, clear-rimmed glasses. We spoke about our travel, and Claire grabbed my hand to pat it. "I don't speak English, but you speak French, so we will be fine," she said generously, even after hearing my poor French. She had such faith in me. After all the explanations regarding the house and promises of a future visit in the morning, we shook hands to say our good nights.

I walked her to the door and said,

"It is a pleasure to meet you. I hope that you will be comfortable to tell me my bad French grammar." I realized that my French was weak to say the least, but I had to construct a sentence I knew how to say. Sometimes in order to make a sentence in French, my English had to suffer. The verb "to correct" was not at the top of my head at that late hour.

She slowly nodded, kept smiling, and said, "*Oui, oui.*"

After she left, I felt like I had finished an exam. "Well, that went well," I said. My husband had a different understanding of the conversation.

"I could be wrong, but I think you just asked Claire to be your bad French grandma," he said. In French, the words for grandma and grammar do sound similar. "Really?" I asked. "Well, we'll see what happens. Either way it's a win for me. If I get an adopted French grandma who corrects my grammar, I'm ahead of the game!"

* * * * * * *

A lot of variables were involved in choosing the perfect French village. Population, services available, rural or urban, climate, amount of tourism, and regional accent all factored into my decision. I narrowed down my choice of regions in France and finally selected the Dordogne Valley. The climate was excellent, and there were more Michelin-starred restaurants in this region than anywhere else in France. Might as well eat well while I'm learning I figured. I spent months and months researching vacation homes on the internet. I was looking for a two-bedroom house in a small rural village that was not on a major tourist route. I wanted to be a unique, approachable object of interest and curiosity.

In the end, Cénac et St. Julien had everything I needed. It was an agricultural town of 1,093 people, tucked around the hill from the UNESCO- protected, famous historical sites of Domme and Sarlat. English-speaking tourists rarely intruded on our life, and we could visit the beautiful sites whenever we wanted. It had just enough businesses that stayed open all year to make life easy, but the commercial sector wasn't so busy as to create traffic congestion. There were many villages in the same area that closed completely during the winter, giving the communities a deserted feeling. It would have been frustrating to try to learn a language if no one were around.

From the very start, I loved my village. It was the perfect size: big enough to have services,

but small enough to be very friendly. Its location had the right balance of rural land with open spaces, and a larger city, Sarlat was close by offering its historical center, movie theater, and shopping opportunities. Cénac et St. Julien was a real, thriving French community, not just a tourist destination. There were two *boulangeries*, each at opposite ends of the main street, to provide a healthy rivalry. During the winter months there were three places to enjoy a cup of coffee and people watch, each with its own personality. Only one shop in town had the governmental license to sell cigarettes. There was a gun shop open only during the weekends of the hunting seasons that routinely left guns in the front display window without any security bars. Happily the village's crime rate was so low that visible firearms were not stolen. Occasionally, the store's mascot, a straw bunny, would hold up a sign in the front window to taunt or insult the hunters. "I will be enjoying the lettuce from your garden tonight. What are you having for dinner?" was the bunny's snide question on the closing day of rabbit season. The Press sold the weekly regional newspaper plus lottery tickets, books, and fishing gear: its most important service to the community though, was as a gathering place to share news and gossip. The local *cave* (wine cellar) sold wine in bottles or in bulk. I felt like I was buying gasoline when buying bulk wine, because the nozzle looked the same. But instead of pumping gas, I was pumping wine, and instead of into a car, it was into a plastic bottle. I liked that, per liter, wine was cheaper than gas. As spring turned to summer, many more businesses opened for the tourist season: three canoe rental huts, a Thai restaurant, the regional food shop, and the *gîte*. (a bed and breakfast inn).

Cénac et St. Julien is on the *Route de Noix*, or Route of Walnuts. Besides the walnuts used in products like walnut oil, liqueur, mustard, and baking, the other crops of the area are corn, tobacco, and sunflowers. Geese and ducks play a large part in the economy, as their livers are made into tasty *foie gras*. The main moneymaking industry has nothing to do with agriculture though: it is tourism. The picturesque towns, Châteaux, gardens, and river offer some of the most beautiful scenery in France. Unusual artifacts from its history still dot the countryside, including enormous millstones and little stone huts with dome-shaped stone roofs called *bories*. Normally a *borie* stands alone in the middle of a field, but very rarely, small groupings of five to seven huts have been found. Their age is unclear, but they are mentioned in written documents prior to

1450. The exact purpose of the huts is unknown, but shelter or storage is the most common hypothesis. The purpose of the millstones is very clear even though they look like the cartoon wheels on the car of the cartoon character Fred Flintstone. Mills along the Dordogne River were an important source of wealth in the 17th and 18th centuries. Cénac et St. Julien had several working mills for the grains and the nuts (walnuts and chestnuts), plus the town-manufactured millstones that were used in the mills in other regions—for mustard production in the Dijon area, and porcelain production in Limoges.

Finally, Cénac et St. Julien had something that I hadn't included in my research, yet I valued so much: a victorious rugby team. I became a loyal fan attending all the home matches and many of the away ones. Sightseeing, rugby, and new French vocabulary made for a pleasing Sunday afternoon.

* * * * * * *

Before arriving in France, I had arranged to have a French teacher who happened to live close to my village, so that French lessons could begin as soon as I arrived. I discovered her by asking my property owner for a teacher referral. When the British homeowner gave me Emma's name and contact information, I telephoned her from California.

"It would be great to have a Californian in class. We don't have one of those. Anyone who is keen enough to come to this cold, godforsaken place in the winter just to learn French is someone I want in my class." Emma said.

"I can't wait to start. I leave in four days and six hours."

Emma began to sing, "I'm leaving on a jet plane. Don't know when I'll be back again."

I didn't know what to say, but she explained.

"I'm known around here as the music director. I'm in a band, and I organize the community's music needs."

Before ending the call, we arranged a meeting place and time for the first day of my French education in Domme.

Starting in the first week, my typical class schedule consisted of ten hours of classes spread over Mondays, Tuesdays, and Fridays. Two of the classes focused on conversation and only French was spoken. The other three French classes emphasized grammar and vocabulary with some French spoken. All of the classes were small; the number of students ranged from only me to eight people, but the average size was four people. The majority of the students were older than I, and all except one Russian woman, had moved to France from England. Most of the students had been taking lessons for many years. It pointed out my naivety to think that three months of lessons would be enough for me to speak French fluently.

Besides French lessons, my plan of attack to learn the language included various strategies. I spent some time figuring out the most common, least threatening, least awkward way to approach strangers in order to have a conversation. It may sound like a simple thing, but picture a stranger who doesn't speak your language coming up to you, wanting to talk. Would that be a highlight of your day, an annoying what-are-you-selling moment, or maybe a bit scary? I reasoned that people walking dogs were good possibilities, especially if I opened the conversation by complimenting their dogs. It always worked.

Then whenever I saw a person working in their well-kept garden, I stopped to compliment their efforts. Very few people hire weekly gardeners like they did in my California community. One day while walking in nearby Sarlat, I spotted an elderly man weeding, so I spoke in French, "Your garden looks perfect. How can you find a weed?" I asked. He quickly stopped what he was doing, threw down his gloves, and came over to the fence to talk. "This rain makes everything grow, especially the weeds. Are you English?" he asked. I was used to this question, and my ready answer was, "No, I am from California." California is the "open sesame" to a conversation. It was perceived as a strange, exotic place that helped make me seem more interesting. We talked about his life in Sarlat and how the city had changed over the years. We both complained about the recent increase of parking fees in the busy downtown area. "I already know where some free spaces are and they are my secret place," I bragged. He hooted with laughter. "All the locals have them and guard that information like where to find truffles. Well, these flowers demand work and care from me all the time, but they are beautiful. They are just like my wife, and they both make me happy," he said. We said our good-byes and thanks to another beautiful garden, a new acquaintance was made.

Cénac et St. Julien's library was another great spot to listen, speak, and of course read French. The community shared the small one-room library located on the elementary school grounds with the school. The back half of the light airy room held the children's literature along with small chairs, plus a large colorful rug for the children to sit on while the teacher read to them. Six floor-to-ceiling shelved sections covered the walls near the entrance, offering novels, magazines, and coffee-table books for the adult visitors. Only one table accommodated those patrons who wanted to linger in the library. The two librarians sat at the only other table in the small room; only theirs was covered in papers and a box labeled "Checked Out Books." The dated but effective system filed the book's index card by the patron's name. The elderly female librarians could have been sisters; they looked that much alike. During one of my visits, they spent an enormous amount of time arranging the picture books before the children's scheduled visit. They discussed the placement of each book, often secretly re-arranging what the other had done. They were equally as patient and thorough with me about answering all my questions. Throughout the four hours on Monday when the library was open, members of the community would come in to visit, gossip, and finally select a book. I didn't mean to be a spy, but listening to their conversation was a difficult, useful drill for me. I would not be surprised if my issued library card that states "Karen – American" were still in the back of the library card box, waiting for me to check out another book.

Another strategy for making friendships was attending rugby matches and cheering on the local team which brought me in contact with a new group of locals. Nothing brought people together more than the sorrow of a close loss or the sweet thrill of a hard-won victory. And every

Tuesday, I shopped at the weekly outdoor market. Several merchants recognized me after just the first week, and warm welcomes were shouted from their food truck. No kisses on each side of the face like long-time friends do, of course I would see if I would ever be accepted that completely. I was at the stage of verbal greetings and a handshake. At least this was one step above the tourist level, which unofficially was ignore them.

Of course media was an easy way to incorporate French into my day. When I was in my car, the radio was tuned to the local talk radio station. I cranked the volume high so I could catch every syllable. I usually drove slowly too, which explains why the local teenagers thought an elderly person was driving down the street. Then French television was a good friend. One channel in particular was a reliable source of clear, articulate narrative, and that was the nature documentary channel.

Not all of my strategies were successful though. I thought a church service would be the ideal place to listen to French. Unfortunately, the sermon was spoken too quickly, and then there was that leg-crossing, uncomfortable feeling, which forced me to stop paying attention. I exited the church service to quickly visit the *toilettes,* planning to go right back into the service. Strangely though, I couldn't find the facilities anywhere, so I asked a woman who was on her way into the church.

"Oh, I recommend behind the hedge over there," she said, pointing towards the neighbor's house, where the couple just happened to be eating their Sunday meal at their picnic table. "But," she continued, "You can pick your own spot of nature. There are good ones on the other side of the church."

I thanked her, waited until she entered the church, then quickly jumped in my car and drove home.

Another unsuccessful attempt was my idea of volunteering at the local elementary school. Silly me went to the school to introduce myself to the principal, but she told me that I must first talk to the mayor to get his approval. I wrote a letter in French explaining my intent, because the odds of my spoken French being strong enough to have an intelligible conversation were slim. In the letter, I introduced myself, asked for volunteer work at the school, and asked if he could refer me to a local teenager who might be interested in being my French tutor. As I stood in front of

City Hall, I gathered my courage, clutched my letter, and repeatedly whispered the correct respectful address for the mayor. I didn't have to worry though. Yes, I met the most powerful, important person at City Hall who tried to help me, but it wasn't the mayor. It was the front desk secretary. She recognized who I was before the front door closed. Still, formal questions had to be asked and answered, like exactly where I was living, who were my neighbors, and how long I would be in her village. As I answered, other employees wandered by to enjoy the show. They were kind as well and joined in when the discussion turned to the oddly foreign concept of volunteering at a school and searching for a tutor. The secretary's head nodded as she re-read my letter. Names were suggested, but each time someone in the crowd would reject the candidate. I could tell they wanted the very best for me, but at the same time, they were not providing any results at all.

"We will keep your letter here and think some more. The school has plenty of teachers, so it is not necessary for you to help," she told me, right before the chorus of *au revoirs*.

Since City Hall couldn't help me, I tried to help myself, but again it led to a dead end. I wrote an announcement for the community board at the only grocery store in the village, asking for a French tutor or conversation partner. I sweated over the choice of words and the tone of the message. After I pinned it to the board, I wondered if I was ready to answer the telephone in French. Turned out I needn't have been concerned, because no one called.

* * * * * * *

As in every culture, there are stages to a friendship or to belonging to a community. In France, a nod of the head, a handshake, and a kiss on the cheek or lips denotes one's ranking in the relationship. This was a touristy area, but I arrived during the wintertime when visitors were rare, which let me skip miles past the tourist level. I shopped at the local stores and ate at the local restaurant frequently enough to be included in the greetings—just at the nod of the head with a personal *bonjour* stage, not to be confused with the public *bonjour* when entering a public place. At first, I had a hard time being bold enough to loudly say *bonjour* as I entered a store. What if people ignored me? Quickly, over the first month, it began to feel comfortable to say it, and eventually it just became good manners. A public *bonjour* was never ignored, because people were polite. When I sat in the restaurant, I watched the greeting process repeat itself over and over. A local came in, travelled from table to table with handshakes for some people and kisses for others - male or female, it did not matter. My table was passed, except for a nod of the head. I wasn't worried. I trusted that there would be time enough to make friendships.

Even the language reflects one's standing in a relationship. There is a formal "you," which is *vous* and an informal "you," or *tu*. I was taught to always use "*vous*" (unless you're talking to a child or animal) until the person invites you to use "*tu*." My neighbors were wonderful people; we visited often, exchanged gifts, and even went through a health scare together, yet in our day-to-day conversations over the first three months, we were still using "*vous*." I wasn't just learning a language—I was also learning a culture.

* * * * * * *

I met Jean-Paul using the garden technique. He and his wife Colette lived at the bottom of the hill. He was often working in his garden or just outside watching life as it passed. His ready smile and quick-witted comments were a welcome addition to my day. He stood at my height about 5' 3", with dark piercing eyes and hands thickly calloused from years of working on his farm. He was an alert, active eighty-year-old man. Since I often parked my car next to his garden, because the parking opposite my house was difficult to access, we had many opportunities to build a friendship. Our first conversation began on the subject of the health of the village trees that lined the narrow roads. He felt the heavy rain was causing the trees to drop their leaves too early. Of course he was curious about me. He politely asked questions to gain enough information to satisfy the questions that would surely come from his wife, who was standing at the kitchen window. When I explained my goal, as well as my love for the French language, Jean-Paul became excited.

"You are a good person. Do you know that my son-in-law who is an American cannot speak French? He does not try!"

"French is very difficult," I lamely offered, since it was obvious that this was a sore point.

"Bah! They have been married many years, and they have a house here. He comes to France all the time, but he does not want to learn."

At the time I didn't know it, but this American son-in-law complaint would be repeated many times to me throughout the year. Hopefully I balanced out his opinion of Americans' ability to learn French, without causing grief around their family's dining table.

Months later, Jean-Paul shared other parts of his life with me as well.

"I was born in this house and have lived here all my life," he told me, after I said how much I liked Cénac et St. Julien. He continued, "My parents spoke Occitan to me and my sisters. I remember when the boy's school was over there and the girl's school was farther in town. I will never forget when the Germans were staying in the manor house on the school's grounds. Look at how close they were to my house. That is something you don't forget." I was honored that he told me about those troubled times, but unfortunately I didn't understand most of his story. I didn't want to blindly ask questions though, because it was too sensitive of a subject. Towards the end of my stay in France when my French had improved, I never could figure out a way to tactfully approach the subject again.

One wintry day, I was walking to my car with the plan to drive into Sarlat for the weekly truffle market. The French Périgord black truffle season starts in December and lasts for two months—if the weather has produced the right conditions for a good crop. Each week during the truffle season, there is an exchange where individuals can bring in their discovered truffles to be weighed and sold to restaurants or the highest bidder. Sometimes the pricey transaction takes place out of the back of a van. It might not seem glamorous, but the expensive fungi and its cousin, the Italian white truffle, are known as the most expensive food in the world. Prices can be as high as $500 for a fourth of a pound. On that day the newspaper didn't make it clear if the public was welcome to observe, but I was going to try.

As I got near to my car, I saw Jean-Paul and we shook hands. Weather was usually our first topic, and after we expressed our disgust with all the rain, he asked where I was going.

"I am going to see the truffle market," I said, showing him the newspaper article. He violently shook his head and waved his finger.

"They will cheat you. It is not a good place for you, because you don't know truffles. And those Italian truffles sneak into the market. I have a friend. Oh, I've known him all my life, and he was born in this town too. He has a truffle dog that can find a truffle like a baby finds milk. This dog is smart. I will call him."

Jean-Paul talked some more, however the fine details of what he was planning went over my head. So I wasn't sure if I would be walking up and down over the hills looking around oak trees, or if I would get to meet this wonder dog, or if nothing would happen at all.

Then as we were standing smack in the middle of the street, having our conversation, a car approached. Claire was the driver, and since she knew both of us, she paused, took her car out of gear so her hands would be free to talk, and joined our discussion. Of course proper greetings were exchanged first. As they expressed their mutual disdain of the truffle market at great length, I noticed occasional traffic, which carefully drove around us. No one honked or made any rude gestures. What a moment! I was standing in the middle of the road in my French village, having a conversation with two new friends. I was living my dream. Sure, I couldn't understand everything that was being said, but that would just make the truffle adventure – whatever and whenever it would be - more exciting.

* * * * * * *

Since this was my year for new experiences, I was hoping for this winter to be filled with snow. A white Christmas was something I'd never had, and it would be the perfect touch for the holidays. Every storm that passed through would raise my hopes for snow, only to have them drenched in a downpour of rain. There were days when snow seemed possible. Many mornings I checked the temperature to find a negative number. I felt quite proud of myself living in below zero conditions; although I must admit, I wore four layers of wool clothes, gloves, scarf, hat, and fuzzy Uggs most of the time, and that was inside the house. I'd always thought a winter scarf was only a fashion accessory. What did I know? My winters were spent in the flat lands of California, where if clouds covered the sun then I thought about building a fire in my fireplace.

A daily morning and evening routine needed to be done in order to survive the cold. It made me feel a kinship to pioneer women. First, I would carry firewood from the below the house, up the steep, cement walkway to the front door, and make a leaning, poorly-stacked pile of the day's firewood under the eaves. If at this point I saw a spider on the wood, I would brush myself off, vow to examine the wood better, and gather my courage for another trip. Stocking wood took a lot of time because of spider duty. The Dordogne Valley was not known for poisonous spiders, but any of those little eight-legged creatures scare me.

heat

thr

use

of

m

b

r

ing the ash from the little, black potbelly stove. The house was
ng room and by an oil burning heating system
oil system was very expensive, so I tried not to
ce the chamber in the stove was clean, I disposed
under the house. Then was the moment for the
rimented with different structures, but I found the
and small pieces of wood on a bed of crumbled
ons was useful too. This source of welcome warmth
ere finished for the day. On a typical winter day, I had
ever lit a fire during a typical morning because I often

rm was simpler. It was just vigilant maintenance of the
reparing boiling water for the hot water bottle. Then
le in my side of the bed, which took an hour to complete.
little baby blue and brown plaid water bottle took away
itched scream that rang from me when getting into the
hristmas gift we bought for our daughters who came to
open the gift early when they arrived in mid-December.
t bedtime.

I tried to do every d to avoid using the oil heating system. For example, the staircase to the second floor was an extremely narrow, beautifully slanted, wooden staircase, with a small opening at the landing. It was easy to hang a wool blanket from ceiling to floor to close the opening, thus trapping the hot air downstairs. But there came a time towards the middle of the winter when we thought it would be wise to buy a little more oil, just in case the fierce snowy storms materialized. The enormous whitish plastic oil tank sat in the back corner below the house, in an above-ground basement, where the firewood, gardening tools, and homeowner's personal items were stored as well. The tank was at least six feet tall and ten feet wide.

People didn't drive up our home's driveway, because it was incredibly steep. Similarly, the narrow lane up the hill behind the house was too steep for me to comfortably drive; however, our one neighbor who lived higher on the hill did drive it and, judging from his speed, had no fear of the drop-off. So I wondered, how would the oil be delivered?

"Do not worry, Karen. They have a special truck with a long …," said Claire, as she used her whole arm to make flat S turns.

"They have a snake?" I guessed, before thinking it through.

"No! It is a …"

This time her arm movement looked like an elephant's nose, but I caught myself before saying that weak guess out loud.

"Wait, please. I have my dictionary," I said, offering it to her.

After a quick search she found the word and showed it to me.

"Oh, of course, a hose."

"And Karen, we do not allow snakes to come into the house," she said with a wicked grin. She added, "I will call the company to make the delivery appointment. Normally it takes a week, but they know me. They will come tomorrow for me. You know I used to drive the ambulance. That's why everyone knows me."

"You did?"

"Oh yes, I drove for many years. My territory was the whole region."

"That's fantastic. So you can drive fast?"

Again that charming, wicked grin appeared with a little chuckle, "I like to drive fast."

What made this exchange so pleasing to me is how much Claire reminded me of my grandma, even though she wasn't quite old enough to be my grandma. Both women were somewhat short, both had clear sparkling eyes, both intelligent, and both women liked to talk fast. I could predict the gradual increase of speed of her words by how many *"exactements"* I elicited. With each agreement, her words came faster, and my grandma did the same thing. But the vehicle similarity was really uncanny. My grandma owned a 1970 Dodge Charger, a muscle car that she loved. She would be at an intersection revving the engine, because she was hard of hearing, but the young drivers in the next car would think the muscle car wanted to race. That is until they saw the grey hair, the blue horn-rimmed glasses, and the barely-can-see-over-the-steering-wheel grandma as the driver. She would surprise them every time by gunning it at the green light. Maybe on my first night in France I had been right to call Claire my grandma?

True to her prediction, my oil appointment was set for the next day. After the noon mealtime, a small flatbed truck with large tank on the platform slowly backed up our shared lane. It was safe to assume that he had had wine with his noon meal, but his driving was exact and safe. He stopped at the top of my driveway and attached the hose to the tank. I couldn't help but think that it did kind of look like a fat snake. Claire turned up at this point and a rapid discussion took place. I bought the minimum amount, which perfectly filled my oil tank to the original mark. It turned out that my careful rationing of the heating oil and generous layering of wool sweaters made the oil last throughout the freezing days of winter.

* * * * * * *

As I was perusing the local newspaper, I saw an invitation to the residents of Domme to hear the mayor give her annual address, called *Voeux du Maire*. It was sort of a State of the Union address for the community given every December with a lively give-and-take with the audience scheduled at the end of the speech, along with a promise of cake. I needed more practice listening to French, and I loved cake, so why not go?

On the Friday night of the speech, there was a massive storm raging. It was raining so hard that the 4:30 p.m. nightfall wasn't discernible, because it was dark throughout the whole day. The wind whipped the branches against the house, and twice I saw a slate roof tile fly off with a particularly strong gust of wind. I had planned to walk up the hill to attend the talk, but the storm caused me to adjust my transportation choice to driving the car. I was still determined to go. I was even a little more concerned that maybe I would be the only one to attend. It would be far too overwhelming if Madame Mayor spoke only to me. It turned out not to be a valid concern though. I was thinking like an apathetic American. In France, it didn't matter that it was a Friday night, it didn't matter that a violent storm was right outside the door, it didn't matter that the evening's entertainment was a political speech: people came. A lot of people came. The population of the village was close to 100, and there were about 60 people who attended. People were very interested in their community's politics. No one was standing close to the cake table except me. Other people were here for the content, not the cake.

The published time to start was 7:00 p.m. Still new to French culture, I arrived at 6:45 p.m., because I left enough time to allow for slow driving in the bad weather, finding a parking space, and locating a sitting place next to the wall. My American cultural background showed that night. No one drove slowly regardless of the storm, no one parked in a designated parking space, just like any other day, and no one wanted to sit down. People spent the first 20 minutes after their arrival walking around the room, greeting their friends and neighbors. Kisses on both cheeks and hearty handshakes were given and received by all ages.

It was getting close to the real start time of 7:30 p.m., so I thought a quick trip to the restroom would be a good idea. I slipped out the side door into the entry hall and accomplished my task, but when I tried to re-enter the hall, I found myself in the greeting line for the mayor. She was personally greeting each voter and spending quality time with each person. This was a French test I didn't want to take only because it would be with the most important person of the village. As I inched forward, I wiped my sweaty palms on my coat and mentally practiced the formal greeting that Claire had taught me just days before.

"*Merci de venir ce soir. Le temps est tres mauvais,*" the mayor began. (Thank you for coming this evening. The weather is very bad)

"*Oui, c'est vrai.*" (Yes, this is true.)

"*Êtes-vous nouvelle à la ville? L'assemblée ce soir sera bien pour que vous puissiez apprendre ce qui est encore accompli et ce qui rester à faire,*" she said. (Are you new to the village? The meeting this evening will be good that you could learn what was accomplished and what still needs to be done.)

"*Je suis très enchantée de faire votre rennaissance, Madame Mayor,*" (I am very happy to meet you, Madame Mayor) I gushed like a groupie, while violently shaking her hand. I was nervous and relieved at the same time. If the event had security guards, the mayor would have called them, because I was not done with my moment with her. "*J'aime toutes les choses que vous faites pour Domme, et je pense que Domme est la plus belle ville.*" (I like all the things that you have done for Domme and I think that Domme is the most beautiful village.)

"*Ah, merci,*" (Ah, thank you) she said graciously, while taking her hand out of my grip.

I found my place by the cake table, and the mayor entered the hall to begin her talk. Everyone stood at attention, listening to her every word about what projects had been accomplished, which projects were almost finished, hopes for future projects, and their costs. The community's death and birth numbers were discussed as well, so people understood the health of the village. Many rural French villages were shrinking, and the threat of a village dying was real. During the whole two-hour address, not one cell phone rang, no one left, not one sigh or snore was heard. People were interested.

There were no angry questions or insults lobbed at the mayor when she finished. Four or five questions were asked about different subjects, which the mayor answered to each questioner's satisfaction, and then the questions ceased. Maybe people were eyeing all the traditional almond cakes being brought to the table.

"Now it is time for this year's king and queen to be found," the mayor said. Wait, I thought, this evening is supposed to be all about democracy. "Please enjoy the cake and good luck," the mayor concluded. And a "let them eat cake"

moment as well, I thought. Did these French people see the irony?

People flocked to the cake table, choosing their piece. Soon I heard cries of "I got it" and "Looks like I'm the king" could be heard. The "it" mentioned was held up for all to see. It was a small, gold-plated coin that had been baked in the cake. Each cake had one hidden in it. The coins signified that the finders would have good luck throughout the rest of the year. Each person was also king or queen for the day, and the paper crown that previously rested on the cake was now put on the finder's head. There were no broken teeth, no choking noises, and no threats of "I'll sue you" were heard, so democracy with a flavor of royalty, all French style, survived once again on a wintry December night.

* * * * * * * *

Nothing makes a house feel more like a home around the holiday time than decorations. We found inexpensive Christmas tree ornaments with glittery silver letters that spelled *Joyeux Noël* on each red glass ball at a French version of a Pier One store. The most traditional Christmas discovery happened at Cénac et St. Julien's outdoor market. It was early Tuesday morning and as I walked into the market, I noticed a new table with a huge homemade sign hanging from it. "Support Your Local School" was printed in block lettering. Six moms were standing around the table ready to sell the homemade Christmas decorations. They had ten-inch straw stars with red ribbon, bunches of mistletoe tied with red ribbon, and homemade treats. They were volunteering at a fundraiser for their children's elementary school, something I had willingly done for many, many years while my daughters were in school. My eyes must have lit up as I rushed towards them, because they all smiled. One said, "Oh, finally here is someone who will help."

"I have done the same thing at my daughter's school for a lot of years. I understand what you are doing."

"I guess schools in every country have to fundraise."

"What will you do with the money?"

" It will be used for trips, so the children can visit the museums and historical places."

I made a purchase, but more importantly I made several friends at that table. I joined them on their Thursday morning power walk up the steep hill to Domme, and one kind, friendly woman and I got together almost every Tuesday to chat in French.

But the house needed more than just our two-foot-high Charlie Brown-like Christmas tree and straw star. Luckily, I had brought Christmas lights from California. We couldn't find lights in the stores, and no other homes in our community had lights outlining their roofline or windows. I thought our lights added joy and warmth to our sweet French home. After the first week that our windows were outlined in bright lights, Claire mentioned them right after we discussed mistletoe.

"Karen, are you afraid to be here?" she asked out of the blue. She patted my upper arm, saying, "It is very safe here. Most people don't lock their doors."

"What? No, not at all. Why do you ask?"

"Well, I saw that your lights were left on all night so I thought, maybe you were afraid."

"Oh, that is for Christmas. The lights make the tree and the house beautiful."

"It is another American custom? Of course. Now that I think about it, I have seen pictures of Las Vegas."

There are other differences in how our cultures celebrate Christmas, the most significant difference being that Santa's visit, or *la fête de Saint Nicholas,* happens on December 6th. That is the day when he brings gifts. Children set their shoes in front of the fireplace for *Père Noël* to place gifts in them. In some regions of France, there is a second Christmas character, *Père Fouettard,* who deals with the naughty children by giving out spankings. Then on Christmas Eve and Christmas Day, the main activities are that family and friends gather together for a religious service and a special meal called *Le Réveillon.* Most churches hold a *Messe de Minuit* on Christmas Eve.

The most traditional Christmas food from the Dordogne is the dessert Yule Log, or *La Bûche de Noël.* It is a sponge cake filled with cream and chestnuts. Our bakery always had several on display during the holidays. They ranged in size and flavor, but the shape of the log remained constant. It is said to represent the logs burned from Christmas Eve to New Year's during the pagan Gaul celebrations. We experienced several celebrations where pagan and religious symbolism were blended in present day celebrations.

There was a different understanding of mistletoe too. Both cultures used it as a decoration; however, in France it is viewed as a good luck charm. I had just hung a small bunch of mistletoe above our door when Claire walked up to the house.

"You will have good luck," Claire told me.

"Do you think someone will kiss me?" I laughed.

"That I do not know, but you are a pretty girl. But you have Steve!"

Somehow the conversation took a weird turn. I found that when confused, asking about what you think is obvious usually helps.

"Claire, do you kiss under mistletoe for a Christmas custom?"

" No. Never. Kissing is for greeting friends or those you love. It is too important to restrict it to a plant or a holiday."

* * * * * * *

S'il Vous Plait, Pouvez-vous Parler Plus Lentement Pour Moi

(Please, Could you Speak More Slowly For Me)

"Come to dinner at 7:30 p.m., and do you drink white or red wine, Karen?" Claire asked me on a rare sunny day in January as we finalized our dinner plans.

"I drink both."

"Very good. Henri is cooking the local specialties for you," Claire said, as she walked away and waved.

This was my first invitation to a French home. It was to be a whole evening without any English; only my hosts' kind patience, wine, and my French dictionary would see me through. At the arranged time, I walked up their driveway as Princess and Gypsy, two little dark, hairy dachshunds barked their *bonjours* and I was greeted by Claire at the open front door. I couldn't help noticing the large, white, gothic styled birdcage with about 15 pigeons in it, right beside the house. Before even putting my foot in the house, I managed to put my foot in my mouth.

"Oh, Claire, you have birds. Do you eat them?" I asked.

Claire looked at me in horror. "No, no, they are champions! I show them. See the medals they have won," she pointed to an impressive number of colorful medallions hanging on the side of the cage. It was their trophy shelf. She went on to clarify, "I am the president this year of the society, the Association *Nationale d'Aviculture,* and our regional show is next month. You should come to see the beautiful birds of France, and there will be bunnies too, but no one really comes for the bunnies. We eat rabbit."

She led me along the house towards the back door, the one where long-time friends enter the kitchen—the door where you step into the heart of the home—and I felt honored. There were warm garlicky smells, and Henri was standing in front of the stove putting the final touches on the meal. He was a short, muscular man who was not afraid to wear an apron tied around his waist when he cooked.

"You will have a real French meal famous for this area," Henri announced.

Henri and Claire's home reflected what was important in their life. In the living room, framed family photos dotted the mantle and cabinet, hunting rifles along with antlers were mounted on the wall, finished knitted sweaters intended for grandchildren sat beside the current knitting project at the edge of the sofa, and numerous doggie toys were tucked here and there. The room was the busy headquarters of the house.

Claire's sister, Lorraine also joined us for the meal. She didn't speak any English either, but she had visited New York City twenty years before. Champagne was poured for everyone and, like families throughout the world, people talked at the same time, laughed at each other's stories, and corrected each other's faulty memories. I had my hands full just to follow the speaker's line of thought.

The first course was ready and we sat down to homemade wild pig paté and homemade deer paté, both garnished with pickles and served with fresh bread. Claire made both of the patés from the kills Henri had made earlier that year. The main course was a mushroom omelette. The mushrooms had been hunted and gathered by Henri earlier in the day.

"I have my favorite places to find the best mushrooms. Claire used to go with me, but she kept picking the poisonous ones. I finally had to stop taking her, because I was spending all my time removing her poisonous mushrooms from our basket and not gathering the good ones," he sighed.

"They look exactly the same," Claire fairly pointed out with a shrug of her shoulders. She continued, "Besides, I grew up in Paris. We didn't pick mushrooms."

Throughout this story, my fork didn't even pause as I ate the delicious omelette. Henri told me he learned to recognize mushrooms as a young boy, taught by his father. He was another man like Jean-Paul who had been born in Cénac et St. Julien and lived there all his life. There were times in his childhood when his skills at foraging fed his family. The next course was the cheese plate with bread. Then came the dessert of chocolate éclairs from the local bakery. It was a feast.

For me, the highlight of the evening was that I could follow the rapid, multi-directional conversation. We covered subjects ranging from what it was like for Claire and her sister growing up in Paris to the benefits of children learning a second language to our past travel adventures. At one point, Claire admonished her sister for talking too fast to me. "But no, she understands every word I say," Lorraine said, giving me way too much credit. Along with our good-byes at the end of the evening, we promised to have dinner again, only next time I would cook an American meal and Henri would teach me how to make the local, traditional garlic soup. That night I was so excited about the whole evening that I literally could not fall asleep. I had a huge smile on my face, and my mind couldn't calm down. I had done it! I had kept up with the conversation. I had been a contributing member, and I'd even understood the jokes. How different this was turning out from my first experience in France when I was a shy, timid 16 years old exchange student living with a gregarious French family. Back then, every day during my two-week stay, I suffered in silence through a three to four-hour dinner, not understanding one word and not saying one word. The host family had mockingly nicknamed me Mona Lisa, because the expression on my face never changed. This year I had a nickname as well, but it was said with affection and a welcoming smile. I was the *petite americaine.*

* * * * * * *

When the refrigerator started making a funny sound one morning, I made a mental note to ask Claire about it since she was my rental property manger. Later that day, I saw her working in her garden. I rang the bell on her driveway gate, rewarded the noisy, affectionate barking of Princess and Gypsy with bacon treats from my pocket, and made my way over to her.

"Bonjour, Claire. *Ca va?*" (Hello, Claire. Is everything okay?)

"*Oui, oui. Il fait froid aujourd' hui, eh?*" (Yes, yes. It is cold today, eh?)

After a little more visiting, I remembered to ask about my problem.

"Claire, my refrigerator makes a crazy sound."

"What makes a sound?"

"My refrigerator."

"What?"

Clearly she did not understand me, even though I said the word with a strong French accent, just like the cartoon character, Pepé Le Pew. The word in question was almost exactly the same in English and French. How could she not understand me? I ended up using my dictionary to show her the word.

"Oh, refrigerator," she said. To my ears, the word sounded exactly like how I'd said it. Well, that's not true. It sounded almost exactly the same. Claire emphasized a different syllable and somehow the word became crystal clear.

During the same afternoon's French class, I asked Emma about the dreaded word.

"No, love. People here shorten it and say refri, but your accent is very good."

"But I was so close. I can't believe she didn't understand."

"It's a dance. The French speak the cha cha. Listen for the rhythm when they speak, and if they step left, heel landing first, then you better land on your heel too. They won't understand ballet."

* * * * * * * *

If a traveler stays in Europe longer than the standard three-month visitor visa, then additional arrangements are necessary. Our trip was going to be at least eleven months, so extra permission was needed. Since we didn't have a company to sponsor us, nor were we likely to become full-time university students, and we weren't going to be illegal aliens, we realized that the long-stay visa was our only option.

The process of obtaining a long-stay visa started in California a year before our departure date. The first step was reviewing the thirty-plus-page application booklet from the Office of French Immigration, which we found online. In it were detailed instructions, clear explanations, and a million forms. The French government wanted to know us in every way. There was the overview form to discover basic information like address, age, education, employment history, passport information, etc. Then documentation was requested to prove our income and wealth. It was a reasonable request, though, because who would want a long-term guest if he/she couldn't pay for their own way? I could also understand the request for a certified copy of our birth certificates, but I wasn't too clear on why the French government wanted a certified copy of our marriage license. We sent it anyway and were thankful that the French bureaucracy monster didn't demand anything harder to supply. They also wanted a return plane ticket or proof of your exit from France as well a notarized letter from us stating that we would not seek employment while in France. I wanted to send along a personalized note saying it would be my pleasure and sole mission not to work at all while in France, but did they have a sense of humor? They asked for three personal references. They wanted a detailed listing of where we would stay each night while in France. Luckily for us, we were renting only one property. They needed to interview us at a French Consulate of our choice. At least six passport-size pictures had to be included in the packet. Our passports had a requirement too; they had to remain current for at least a year after our departure from France.

Of course there were non-refundable fees associated to obtaining a visa. And we had to prove we had medical insurance coverage during our stay in France. Last but not least, the government wanted to make sure visitors were healthy; again, totally understandable. Health questions were answered by submitting a complete history of vaccinations and past illnesses in the visa packet. After arriving in France, a physical exam would be given by a French doctor. The doctor would have the power to immediately rescind the visa if one of us failed the exam. The French medical exam would have to be done within the first 30 days after our arrival. Well, more accurately, we would have to notify the Office of Immigration within the first 14 days of our arrival in France. They would mail back a standardized receipt to us stating that they received it. The French clock to the 30-day deadline would still be ticking while we waited for the next step. It would be scarier then, because we knew that they knew that we were in their country. Finally, the sweetest form letter would arrive to inform us of the date, time, and place of our medical appointment. There would be no second choice of date, no "please let us know if this date doesn't work for you" in the text. It would be in our best interest to be at this appointment.

But I have stepped ahead in the process. Back in California, months before the trip, we collected information, made copies of tax returns, wrote intention letters and had them notarized, collected medical information, took awful passport pictures (the woman would not let me smile) and asked our most articulate friends to be personal references. (Weeks after mailing in the application, our friends told us that the French government did contact them to ask about us. They reasoned that, at the very least, French perfume or French chocolates were owed them as payment for their "lies.")

Once the application packet was complete, with one set of originals and two complete sets of copies, the interview in the San Francisco office was scheduled. There was a time element to the interview as well. It had to be completed within 30 days of the date of travel. The only tricky part was that the Office wanted to keep all three sets of the application—including all the originals, our plane tickets, and our passports. They promised the documents would be returned in plenty of time before travel. I had to trust them.

The interview at the French Consulate in San Francisco was very casual, quick, and concise. We stood at a drab counter in the style of a past-its-prime dentist office, handed in the packet, and paid the fees. The clerk compared our passport to our faces.

"Why do you want to stay so long in France?" she mildly asked in English with a heavy French accent.

I was expecting the interview to be conducted in formal French in a dark, walnut-paneled office, with only heavy, gold-framed mirrors, ornate crown molding, and the French flag as decoration. I thought the representative would drill question after question at us instead of being quite pleasant.

"Well, I have always wanted to speak French and I love France," I began. She wrote some notes in her section of the form.

"I'd like to learn more about the culture, but really, this trip is about learning the language."

I was ready to go on, but she leaned over the clipped, ink-marked counter and handed us a receipt for the fees.

She smiled without making eye contact and said, "*Merci*, and good luck."

It was pretty painless.

Fast forward to me standing at my mailbox in Cénac et St. Julien, clutching my sweet, sweet form letter two months later, and reading it with my French dictionary in hand. It had our medical appointment date and time, but there at the bottom of the page were new requests for information added by the French government. In beautiful prose, they asked to review our passport, medical form, letter of admittance, and—a new requirement—submit a post-marked envelope and letter from the electric company to prove where we live. This request would be difficult to fulfill because we were renters who didn't pay an electric bill. That bill was sent to England to the British homeowner.

There was only one person to go to for help with this problem. The person who understood French bureaucracy better than most French people and who knew how the French mind worked: Emma, my French teacher.

"I was thinking of writing a letter explaining that I don't own the house, but I could give them a copy of the rental agreement with the rental dates," I said.

"No, that won't work. Too straightforward," Emma said, shaking her head.

"What am I going to do? I have to get this visa." It was already January and my visitor visa would run out in February.

"Here's what you do: you out document them. Those bastards love paperwork. So write to the owner of the house and have him make a copy of the photo page of his passport. Then he makes a copy of the electric bill with the address of the French property showing. Then he writes a letter stating that he owns the house in France. That should make them happy. What a pain in the ass for you, but welcome to France."

On the day of the medical appointment, we made the two-hour drive to Bordeaux with all our documents in hand, well, two hands because there were a lot of documents, and we waited at the door of the Office of Immigration. Our appointment was set for 11:47 am, which I found odd because it was so dangerously close to the beloved meal hour. Nine other visa applicants waited along the curb and sidewalk with us. Six languages were whispered in nervous conversations as we killed time waiting for the office to open. At exactly 11:45 a.m., a woman dressed in smart business casual arrived, unlocked the door, and started the visa application procedure by handing us a form to complete. Would the forms ever end?

I was the first person called into the examination room. Before any questions or pokes or prods, the woman asked me to undress. She handed me a white paper vest that came to my knees, but didn't tie or close in any fashion.

"Leave it open in the front," she said. "But don't worry, we only are going to the next office."

Of course that office was on the other side of the waiting room, making it necessary to walk through the waiting room. When I was as ready as I ever would be, I clutched the sides of the vest together in the critical places and tiptoed quickly across to the x-ray room.

After the x-rays were taken, two French doctors met with me, all of us fully clothed, and I'm proud to say both consultations were conducted completely in French. The first doctor reviewed my chest x-ray to look for any signs of tuberculosis. She said my lungs were perfectly clear and congratulated me on my health. I told her about my three seasons of backpacking the Pacific Crest Trail, which starts at the Mexican border and ends at the Canadian border, exactly 2,650 miles away. Of course I didn't say it that elegantly in French. My exact words were "I walked a long, long time in the mountains. I slept on the earth and carried all my things. I went from Mexico to Canada and it was 2,650 miles". She was impressed, asked questions about the trip, and most importantly, gave me an official stamp on my document. Then the second doctor asked general health questions like if I smoked, how much did I exercise, and how much did I drink. My answer of two to three glasses of wine per week caused her to say, "That is not very much." Again I got the all clear from the second doctor, so that left only one more meeting - with the governmental official from Immigration who was in the third office. She reviewed the documents I brought to the meeting, and I held my breath when she came to the electric bill paperwork. She read them over twice then looked at me.

"I have the rental papers for the house if you would like to see them," I offered. In my hand were the forty pages of the rental contract. Emma told me the French love paperwork.

"Oh, no thank you. I think this explanation is sufficient," she said, as she issued the long-stay visa.

I had done it! I'd out-documented the masters of the game and received my visa.

* * * * * * *

As I walked up the hill towards my house, after my second French class of the day, Jean-Paul spotted me. Not bothering to wait until he was closer to me, he yelled, "I talked to my friend. The truffle dog will be ready on ...," he violently waved his arm like he was throwing a baseball then he finished his sentence, "Monday."

"That is great. Next Monday?" I guessed. Being an excellent charades player was so useful when learning a language.

"Yes, next Monday. Be ready."

"Okay. What time?"

"The dog doesn't know. I'll talk to my friend again. Could be morning or afternoon."

The tricky part about these arrangements was that Jean-Paul didn't have my phone number or know where I live. Come Monday, I wasn't sure how I would know when to meet him or exactly what we would be doing. When I mentioned this concern to my mom during our regular Skype session, she reassured me. "Karen, it's a small town. I bet most of the locals know exactly who you are and where you live." Regardless, I had a feeling that the dog knew more than I did.

* * * * * * *

Several times a week, I hiked the steep, one-mile climb up the backcountry one-way lane to Domme, situated on the top of the hill overlooking the Dordogne River, to attend my French classes. It was a paved shortcut that only the locals used; it allowed them to avoid the tourist traffic in the summertime. I imagined the writer Henry Miller strolling up my hill, and I could understand why he made the comment that this area was "… the nearest thing to Paradise on Earth." I agreed with him.

Domme is a well-preserved medieval *bastide* village that has the entire outer wall with several gates intact. During the Hundred Years' War, the community changed hands many times between the French and the English, but the village's oldest historical evidence dates to between 1307 and 1318, when the imprisoned Templar Knights carved graffiti in their tower cell. Using rudimentary sharp objects, they meticulously carved a detailed, lace-draped altar into the stonewall facing the sunrise for their prayers, and around the cell numerous Templar crosses were found.

Once I arrived in Domme, I had to do a bit more climbing to reach my classroom in Emma's house. Her wooden, spiral, slightly tilted staircase to our attic one-room classroom had piles of books, shoes, and plants sharing the narrow space. The room itself was an eclectic mixture of educational materials, stuffed animals, religious artifacts, stacks of books, and wine glasses piled around the edges of the room. A large wooden table occupied the center of the space, which we shared during lecture.

The first time I met Emma, she had me pause by her front door and gave me a warning.

"Before you go into my house, I should tell you that I don't like to do housework and oddly enough my husband doesn't seem too happy to do it either. So don't let the mess scare you."

Emma had a thick, heavy English accent being from the rural, coal mining area of Manchester, England. Her English was salted with swear words and her French sounded smooth and perfect with the sexy French "r"s. When Emma was nine years old, her parents bought the house in Domme, and every year her family holidayed in France. At a young age, Emma had an ear for languages like her father. Coupled with her outgoing personality and curiosity, she learned French quickly just from her friends in the village. She continued to study French at university in England; often at oral exams she knew more than the professors. She had a solid understanding of how to be successful.

"I knew how to play the game. I wanted the bloody degree, so I kept my mouth shut when they made a mistake in French. I could have told them that no one in France would say it their way. They sounded like British idiots with awful accents."

When she finished her degree, she knew she wanted to live in France full-time. She left England and, according to her, never regretted it.

After a month of lessons, I boldly brought my love of games to class.

"What do you have, Karen?" Hazel asked. Hazel was a sweet, proper, soft-spoken British woman who usually bought a bottle of wine to class for us to share. Her eyes and hair were the soft brown color of a hazelnut, which helped me remember her name at a time when I had many new names to learn.

"It looks like she brought her recyclables. Do you have your rubbish too?" Sue asked me. Sue was a fast-talking, British lady who always wore loud colors and had unlimited stories about her grandchildren and her garden. She was rightly proud of both.

"No, this is the world premier of a game I created called Verb It, and you ladies are the lucky guinea pigs," I said.

The game was drawn on a large, wrinkled piece of cardboard, so I could forgive the trash comment. I had spent the prior weekend drawing a Monopoly-like board, except in place of properties, verb groupings were scattered. Instead of chance cards, I wrote unique verb-related challenges.

"Is it a drinking game?"

"We can drink during any game, so of course it's a drinking game. How does it work?" Emma asked.

I set up the board, gave everyone a playing piece, and explained the game's rules at the same time. I knew that my classmates already understood that French verbs were grouped by the spelling of the infinitive form. The largest number of French verbs have a 'er' ending. They are the most straightforward and easiest to learn how to conjugate because they follow a

constant set of rules. The second group has its own unique rules and is recognized by their 'ir' ending. The most difficult group would be those which end in 're'.

"It's a teaching tool to learn French verbs. If you land on a red square, you conjugate a 're' verb of your choice in the past, present, and future. The green squares are for 'er' verbs, and the blue squares are for the 'ir' verb group. You also have to say the English meaning. Do you guys want to play?"

There was a chorus of "Hell, yes!" "Oh, yes!" and "Sure!" So the game began.

"I'll be the referee and god-like judge, so there will be no cheating," Emma announced.

"Karen, I noticed that there are a lot more 're' spaces than the others," Hazel said.

"Well, they are the hardest ones, I think, so I wanted more practice with them."

Emma nodded her approval.

"Those are the ones you could live a real life with. You can read, live, fry, make, believe, deduct. Remember, the 're' verbs were the ones Victor Hugo used whenever he could. His writing is richer because of 're' verbs," she said.

"Hazel, would you like to roll the dice first?" I asked.

"Oh, I'm nervous, but here I go."

There was a lot of laughter, no swearing, and no cheating. The ladies were creative with their verb choices, especially since repeating a verb was not allowed. They never opted for the obvious easy choice, even though there were times when being put on the spot drew a blank mind.

"Oh, I can't think of another verb ending in 'ir.' Give me a hint," Sue asked.

"Well, I COULD if I MUST," I stressed trying to help although Sue's bright neon orange dress was a bit distracting.

"CHOOSE carefully," Hazel added.

"FINISH your turn," Emma said.

"Oh, thank you. Now I have too many to choose from."

By the end of the class we all felt we had learned some new verbs.

* * * * * * *

You know you've been accepted as a friend when a French person kisses you as part of the ritual of saying hello. It is a special greeting. Special in that it means you've passed the barrier of being an outsider. The number of kisses on the cheek varies by country; in France usually two kisses, one to each side of the face are given whereas in Belgium three kisses are exchanged by returning to the first side—although this is just a general norm. It doesn't matter if it's the start of a community meeting or parents dropping off their children at school, people take the time to greet each other with a kiss, a handshake, or a nod of the head. I was very happy the day I realized that I needed to leave my house at least twenty minutes earlier than when I'd first arrived in Cénac et St. Julien, just to allow time for the greeting process. I was finally a member of the kissing community.

My first kiss from a French friend was from Claire in January. I was walking up the hill past her house, with my arms full of packages from the outdoor market, when she saw me. She was working in her garden with her little dogs beside her, who were digging in the dirt as much as she was. All of them came up the driveway to greet me, and without either of us thinking about it, Claire and I kissed hello. It was normal for Claire. For me it was a wonderful breakthrough.

I have to admit, I became a bit of a kiss snob. My British friends in the French classes were very kind and kissed me hello as soon as I joined the class. Yet I had done nothing to earn their kiss; no time towards the friendship had been invested. Somehow a kiss from a French person meant more to me, because I had passed a test of time and shared experiences to advance our friendship to a new level. A month earlier, I received a polite hello, but now I was kissed just like an established local. There still was a wide communication gap due to my poor French. But isn't it great that a kiss says you're a friend in any language.

* * * * * * *

35

One special morning I got up at 2:45 a.m. I had worn my daytime clothes to bed, so I could quickly get ready for my visit to the local *boulangerie*. I knocked at the bakery door at 2:55 a.m. Chef and his two assistants were already there, hard at work. The trays of croissants were rolled and ready to go into the oven. The *pain au chocolat* were filled, looking good enough to eat raw. The week before while I was standing in line waiting to buy my morning croissant, Chef had invited me to observe the workday of making bread for the community and the surrounding area. A baguette and a croissant are the quintessential symbols of France, and since I loved bread I jumped at the chance to see behind the scenes of an exceptional *boulangerie*.

It was surprising how physical the whole process was. Chef and his assistant hauled the large flour bags across the room like firemen carrying bodies, continuously lifted heavy trays, manhandled the hot, large oven racks, and remained on their feet throughout the night and early morning hours. They had to maintain a steady pace in order to finish all the batches in time for the first customers when their doors opened at 7:00 a.m. Maybe that was why Chef was lean and muscular. It just didn't seem possible to me that the creator of such delicious, sugary goodness could be without any excess fat, but he looked great. There was friendly banter and joking between Chef and the assistants, but when Chef's tone of voice changed to give instructions, both assistants immediately said, "*Oui, Chef*" and went into action. Chef was trained as an artisan *boulanger, pâtissier, chocolatier, glacier*, and a *confiseur*. Each skill takes years and years of study and training. He had trained in Paris and had owned this bakery for over ten years.

Chef told me that bread was the most important part of the meal. His recipe for dough had the right balance of flour to water, which gave the bread substance yet did not leave the person with a heavy feeling after eating it.

"That so-called bread in the big grocery stores is nothing but water. There is no soul in it," he said. I asked if there was a season with higher bread consumption and he smiled. "The French

must have their bread all year long," he said. There were seasonal breads though. For example, around Easter there were special rolls and small loaf breads made with anise.

I watched as breads in different shapes and flavors were pushed and pulled from the oven. When the tenth batch of dough was being made in a huge mixer that looked like a hot tub, I asked if it was for tomorrow. "No, bread should be eaten on the day it is made," his assistant said. His tone of voice implied that I was a barbarian to even ask such a question. Chef told me that it was just from experience that he knew how much bread to make. People from miles away drove to Cénac et St. Julien for his bread, and he also made the bread for the hospital/senior center and for some restaurants.

The bakery was divided into three large rooms. There was the storefront, decorated showroom, with a wall of breads and four glass cases that displayed the cakes and candies where customers entered to make their purchases. The middle room was the kitchen for candy, cakes, macaroons, and pastries. Then the back room was the large super-clean, tiled area where the breads were made. The oven took up most of the space in this room, because it was a large floor-to-ceiling, steel-framed box, filled with four long racks that could be pulled out across the length of the room, usually one at a time. Other equipment, like the 3' x 5' mixers and 6' rolling racks, was moved around the room as necessary to make workspace.

The heavenly smell of fresh baked bread, the camaraderie of early morning hours, and the beautiful sight of all that bread made waking up early so worth it. The eight hours I spent observing the team transform flour and other ingredients into a variety of delicious products was as satisfying to me as if I had made breakfast for the whole community. My hands never touched any dough except when holding my breakfast of a hot-out-of-the-oven *pain au chocolat* that Chef kindly gave to me, but for a day I still felt like one of the kitchen crew. I also liked combining chocolate with learning new French words. Why hadn't I thought of that earlier?

* * * * * * *

It seemed like it was always raining this winter. It was an extremely wet year, with no promise of letting up. Typically, the normal rainfall during the year is 750 mm— an average of 112 days of rain—and it looked like we were off to a good start to beat the norm. Little did I know at the time, but in the forthcoming summer, when rainfall should remain at a constant zero percent, the precipitation in June would be 47mm (1.85 inches), in July 42 mm (1.65 inches), and in August 41 mm (1.61 inches). The soggy weather caused one reporter on the nightly news to close his report by saying, "This weather is not my fault. It is going to rain, and I don't want to hear complaints or threats. It's not my fault."

When we woke to the fifth consecutive day of a downpour, we decided to venture out into the storm for the perfect rainy day activity: visit one of the famous prehistoric caves of the Dordogne Valley. The choices of world-class, Cro-Magnon cave art were impressive, making the decision of where to go a difficult one. Grotte de Rouffignac featured 10,000 to 13,000-year-old sketches and engravings on the walls and ceiling of the cave, predominantly of prehistoric elephants or woolly mammoths, although horses, bison, ibexes, and even rhinoceroses were represented too. Then the renowned cave Lascaux II offered an exact reproduction of 15,000-year-old bulls, horses, and reindeer.

We were confident that at some point during our year we would eventually visit most of the caves, so by mid-morning we selected Grotte de Font-de-Gaume in Les Eyzies. Once the decision was made, we leisurely got ready and casually drove over to the cave. The tree-covered parking lot was completely empty, causing us to double check the operating hours. Did we make the beginner's mistake of arriving during the two-hour lunch break? No, it was early afternoon, not a French holiday, not the wrong address, and not during a strike, so the only thing to do was enter the visitor's office. The two women working in the ticket and gift shop were happy to see someone and congratulated us on coming out on this rainy day.

"May we visit the cave?" I asked, still not believing no other visitors were around.

"Of course. Robert, your tour guide, is waiting in the next hut along the path. He will be happy to start your tour when you arrive. Two other visitors are already there," she said.

It was almost like having a private tour of the authentic 15,000 to 18,000-year-old cave art. The four of us plus our guide entered the cave through a locked, steel gate, and we felt the temperature drop dramatically as we stepped deeper into the cave. Robert used the flashlight to highlight the examples of bison and incomprehensible symbols. He rapidly moved the light over the herd of bison to create the illusion of movement. He explained that archeologists believe that the flickering torches originally used by the artists provided this sense of movement to the paintings. It was interesting to see how the painters used the natural curve of the rock to emphasize the animal's strength and speed. The beauty and the unbelievable age of the paintings made this experience memorable. Robert patiently explained the art techniques, the history of the cave, and how it survived through the world wars and through current conditions. After the tour, I thanked Robert and off-handedly mentioned how glad I was that we decided to visit, almost on a whim.

"You have no idea what a rare occurrence today is," he said.

"What do you mean?"

"My wintertime tours usually have more people than this, and in the summertime, it is crazy."

"I can imagine."

"It is no exaggeration to say that there have been fistfights among the people waiting in line for tickets. I have seen it. Well, there are so many people who want to visit the caves, but it is very important for us to protect the art. It is a national treasure. There used to be a limit of 160 visitors per day, and then in 2013 the number was reduced to 80."

"It is very difficult to visit the cave?"

"We created a simple system, where visitors must buy the ticket the same day as their visit, and they must be in line to receive the ticket. When we have sold 80 tickets, we close the window. Simple and elegant, no?"

"No problem."

"Oh, but there were problems. People would let their friends wait at home or in the car, but the person waiting ten people behind him did not know that. When he counted the people ahead of him in line, he believed that he was within the 80-person limit. Then Katherine would announce that the ticket window would open in ten minutes, and tickets would only be sold to people who were standing in front of her. Oh, many phone calls were quickly made telling friends to hurry down, and people would rush to their cars to get family members. Now, all of a sudden, the line would grow, and the man previously within the limit was pushed far behind."

"There was a fight?"

"Picture a huge fight in our parking lot, men and women screaming at each other. Punches were thrown." He shook his head, recalling the pathetic event. "We blamed the people from Paris; but really, man has not come that far since Cro-Magnon times."

"I am so happy to be here in the wintertime."

"And it is good you visited the cave this year, too. We believe it is highly likely that in the near future, the cave will be closed to the public. The paintings are delicate."

"They are extremely beautiful. Thank you again for a wonderful tour."

* * * * * * *

An interesting way to learn more about a country is to review their expressions. There is a pleasing pattern of food that appears in many of the French sayings:

- Mind your own onions	- Mind your own business
- A look that could burn	- An evil look
- You are the butter on my spinach	- A term of endearment
- He has hairy hands	- He is lazy
- To arrive like a hair in the soup	- If a remark in a conversation is irrelevant
- To have a cat in your throat	- They use cat instead of frog
- To have a blue fear	- To have a bad scare
- It is worth its weight in peanuts	- It is priceless
- To break down open doors	- To state the obvious
- To have an ass full of noodles	- To be lucky
- It's in the pocket	- They use pocket instead of bag
- To suck the dandelions by the roots	- To be dead
- Don't sell the bearskin before killing it	- Don't count your chickens before they hatch
- I see you coming with your big clogs	- Now we are finally getting to the point
- The cow!	- Expression of surprise
- Did not invent gunpowder	- To be a little dumb
- Comb the giraffe	- To do something useless

* * * * * * * *

Every day, I tried to incorporate a French lesson—either in a formal classroom or in everyday life. Exceptional days were when I had lessons in both worlds. One day, my classroom was an auction house and the lesson was French numbers. Numbers were a bit tricky for me, because I had to do some math while speaking French. In French, there are no unique words for the numbers between seventy and ninety-nine: they are compounded numbers made up of smaller numbers. For example, the word for 80 is four-twenty and for 97 is four-twenty-seventeen and the word for 73 is sixty-thirteen. French pre-schoolers learn the compound numbers by rote in sequence with the smaller numbers without having to understand any arithmetic, but most English speakers like me have to perform some quick mental math to get to the compounded numbers.

I noticed that when I needed to say a number in French, it was easy for me. The difficulty occurred at those times when someone else unexpectedly said a number to me in the middle of a conversation. My mind panicked and became distracted by the arithmetic. I tried to simultaneously translate the number by doing the necessary math, while still keeping up with the conversation flow. The brilliance of attending several weekly Friday afternoon auctions at the Sarlat auction house was that the auctioneer provided a steady stream of numbers, so I could practice without any conversation getting in the way. It worked very well: almost too well, because I went home with three items from the auction.

I purposely sat in the last row of the mismatched chairs for the maximum best viewing of the room and crowd, but also so I could sneak out when my brain became exhausted. I had almost reached that point of needed exit, when I noticed the assistant carrying my greatest weakness to the podium. Even from across the large room, I knew I wanted those items. Wanted them enough to overcome my fear of raising my hand to bid. The assistant carefully balanced three red wine crystal goblets on a tray, as he placed them by the podium to be the next item up for bid. Each goblet had a 2-inch band of a different soft color around the rim of the glass. They looked like Venetian glass, and the bands of color were sky blue, mint green, and rose.

When the bidding began, I realized that I hadn't pre-registered, so I didn't have a professional paddle with a number. Not a problem. Earlier I had seen other people raise their hand, and then if they won the item, they just registered afterwards. The bidding for all three glasses began at 40 euros. Another woman got the nod from the auctioneer's head. Fifty euros were offered by a different bidder and quickly accepted before I had had the chance to do anything except the translation. By the time I decided that 80 would be my line-in-the-sand, hard, fast limit, the first woman had dropped out of the bidding, and the current asking price was 80 euros. "*Moi!*" I shouted, as I stood up with hand in the air. Where had all this courage come from? My heart was beating so fast. A few people politely laughed at my enthusiasm and beginner's style.

"Oh, madame really wants these glasses. They are beautiful," the auctioneer said. Maybe it was my accent, or maybe it was standing up that conveyed I was determined to have these glasses no matter what the cost, because at 80 euros, the glasses were mine.

The other perfect, real-life event for learning numbers was the monthly fundraiser *loto*. *Loto* was the French version of bingo, except there were luxurious prizes and the snacks were chocolate crêpes with good French wine. Again, the need to listen to someone announcing numbers in a rapid manner, when I only had to concentrate on the math, helped me a great deal. It was a bit humiliating when one *loto* card was all I could handle; most of the eighty year olds with thick reading glasses and hearing aids were easily tracking fifteen cards.

Finally, the grocery store clerk helped me learn numbers as well. I stood at the checkout counter with the clerk ringing up each item, sometimes visiting with me, but often silent. Just before the grand total was announced, I would turn my eyes away from the display. It was important to listen to the number and try to understand it without reading it.

"Here is the number, madame," the helpful clerk said, turning the bright yellow digital number towards me.

"But that is not playing with honor. Each time I try to understand without looking."

"Good for you. Okay, next time I will say every price of each item for you."

She was my favorite clerk and I looked for her each time I went to the store. The other checkout clerk was kind, but she had a habit of chewing gum, which destroyed her pronunciation.

* * * * * * *

Claire, Henri, and I were looking at the calendar trying to find a date when they could come to dinner at my house. I was going to cook an American meal, and no, it would not involve a hamburger. Claire pointed to Friday, February 14th, as a possibility.

I either said "St. Valentine's" too softly or incorrectly, because Claire said, "It is a good day, no?"

I wanted to make sure they didn't mind having the dinner on St Valentine's Day, so I half-jokingly said, "But Friday is the day of love."

They both looked at me strangely in a heavy, prolonged period of silence. We suggested other dates, but there was always a conflict. The 14th seemed to be our best option.

"Well, okay, but it is a special day of love that which is St Valentine's," I said.

"Ohhhh, St. Valentine's!" Claire and Henri both exclaimed. "No, that day is nothing. Maybe I'll get a rose," Claire said, as she wrote our dinner date on the calendar.

Later that evening when I was back at my house, I realized in horror (although I was laughing out loud) that they must have thought I was making a comment about their private love life on Fridays. Oh, the joys of learning a new language and the fun of making mistakes.

* * * * * * *

A dozen long-stemmed red roses arrived for me with a very romantic note from my husband, who was in New Zealand. My husband is a great guy, and I could tell he really applied himself when writing this note. Man, France is having a good effect on him," I thought. When we Skyped later, I thanked him for the flowers and gushed about the poetic note. After reading it to him, he agreed that it was very romantic—except the only words that he could take credit for were *"Je t'aime."* The French flower shop must have thought Steve needed a little more spark, so "Born on my lips and my heart, I love you," was added to the message. I had to admit, France truly was the country of love.

* * * * * * *

I knew I was learning, but sometimes it felt like I was learning how much I didn't know. For example, for years I used the word "chaque" to mean "each," which was correct when it is used as an adjective. However, now I learned that there were two other ways to say "each" in French that

I had never known, which is "chacun" and "chacune". These are the masculine and feminine "each" when used as a pronoun. I also discovered that there are two ways to form the past tense of the word 'had': one is *passé compose,* "have had" (*j'ai eu*), which refers to completed actions, and the other is *imparfait,* as in "had" (*j'avais*) for habitual or continuous actions in the past. For a quick reference and learning tool, I made a deck of homemade verb flashcards that I carried with me at the bottom of my bag. The flashcards had French on one side and the corresponding English meaning on the other. One day, while I waited for my meal at a restaurant, the waiter noticed me studying the cards.

"What do you have?" he asked.

"I made these to learn French verbs."

"That is wonderful. Okay, I will test you. If you are correct all the time, I will bring a special dessert."

"But if I am wrong, do I get no dessert? Maybe this is too dangerous."

"Have courage!"

But then he added under his breath, "Anyone who takes the time to learn my beautiful language deserves a special dessert."

Some French verbs are extremely exact; there is a verb that means, "bored while standing in a line". As in English, a verb often has more than one meaning. To discuss and to argue is the same word in French, which begs the questions what does this say about the French that they make no distinction between a discussion and an argument? What does it say about English-speakers that we do? Likewise, the same word is used for to smell and to feel. How the verb is used in the sentence will clarify its meaning. My favorite double meaning in one verb was *rendre*. It means to give back, to return (something), to render, and to vomit. I thought that was the ultimate in giving something back.

Another quirk of the French language was it would be impossible to have this discussion in French even if a prior discussion had taken place referring to the action:

"Will you?"

"I will!"

"I would."

"Do."

It's not because it is too concise or may seem too pushy. This fictional conversation is not possible in French because the future and conditional tenses are each constructed by adding a suffix on to the root verb. There is no word for "will" as a verb or "would."

Emma pointed this out after class one day, while we sat on her terrace with her two hens, William and Harry, foraging around our feet. She finished rolling her cigarette and remembered.

"My son is French, but he learned English at a young age. It tickled him to randomly shout out in English, "Will you?" and then we'd have this bizarre conversation and laugh. Philip (Emma's French husband) had no fucking idea what we were going on about."

* * * * * * *

The goal was to cook a delicious Valentine's Day dinner for Claire and Henri that represented America, but would also fit within Claire's special diet, since she was diabetic. Hamburgers were out of the question, just too informal. Apple pie would be nice; however, the amount of sugar in a pie would be a problem. A turkey would be too much food, and it would be difficult to find one in the markets. No other food screamed out "America" to me, but I came up with a theoretical menu and decided to explore the Friday outdoor market in another village to see if my menu would work. I was thinking of artichoke and goat cheese squares as a first course, stuffed bell peppers with green salad and garlic bread as the main course, and mixed fruit as the dessert.

There was a rich selection of vegetables at the three veggie stalls. I had selected two green bell peppers and two red ones, a red onion, and two bulbs of garlic, when I noticed the pale orange pumpkins. They were a variety that I didn't recognize.

"Is this squash good to make squash bread?" I asked the owner of the stall. I didn't know the word for pumpkin.

"That is not possible."

"Well, is the other squash better?"

"No. Pumpkin is not bread. I have never heard of such a thing."

He said it so firmly that even I started to doubt the existence of the yummy bread. Worse, though, was being so anxious over his abruptness that I didn't notice the French word for pumpkin. The rest of my shopping went smoothly, buying the meat, bread, and fruit.

Preparation for the meal actually started on Thursday. I saved my bread from the bakery, so it would be stale enough on Friday to make breadcrumbs for the filling in the bell peppers; I cleaned the house, top to bottom; I walked to the store to buy the beverages; and I made the artichoke and goat cheese squares.

On the Friday evening of the dinner, Claire and Henri arrived at the requested time. The 6:00 p.m. dining hour I had set was American too. I was sure they felt like dinner was being served in the middle of the afternoon.

I put their gift of a thick bunch of bright yellow gentians in water and then poured each of us a glass of champagne.

"Oh, how nice, champagne," Claire said. She took a sip and smiled.

"Now the American influence will start," I said. I reached into the refrigerator and took out the orange juice. They looked puzzled.

"We drink champagne with orange juice," I said.

I didn't hear a gasp from them, but I noticed Claire, probably unconsciously, moving her glass slightly away from me.

"It is really very good. Would you like to try?"

"Yes, of course we will try."

"That would be very interesting. Thank you."

We visited over drinks, and I served the first course. When it was time to refill our glasses, we stayed with pure champagne. They enjoyed the squares, even asked for seconds, and they were fascinated with the stuffed bell peppers. It was the first time they had seen a bell pepper prepared in such a way. Again, they requested seconds. Now we were at the point in the meal when a cheese plate was customarily served in a French home.

"I do not have a cheese plate, because this is an American meal. We eat our cheese in other ways, like in the squares," I said.

"That is not a problem. Everything was excellent," Henri said.

"Cheese is important, but seeing how other people eat is interesting too," Claire said, "Besides, we have cheese at home."

The fruit salad was served in frosted wine glasses, which pleased them. I pointed out another American trait of serving coffee with the dessert. They never drank coffee, so it was a moot point.

At the end of the evening, as they bundled up in coats and scarves, after our kiss good night, Claire said, "This was the first time I had a meal in this house, and I am so happy that it was an American one with you."

* * * * * * *

It had been raining steadily for weeks and weeks. Most of the fields looked like lakes, and the mud was thick. I wondered how Jean-Paul, his friend, the talented truffle dog, and I would fit in

Jean-Paul's friend's little truck. Before the hunt would not be an issue, but what about afterwards, when all of us were muddy? Did I want to have a muddy dog on my lap? Did I really want to put Jean-Paul's friend in the position of making a Sophie's Choice-like decision of who would sit in the back of the truck? I had never found a truffle in my life. The odds for a comfy seat were not in my favor.

It turned out that there wasn't a problem, because Jean-Paul and his friend realized it was too muddy to go on a hunt. All of us were to meet at Jean-Paul's house on Friday, after my second French class. Unfortunately, on that day my class ran long, so I missed the appointed hour. I ran down the hill to Jean-Paul's house to apologize and found that they had kindly arranged to try again the next day. So much suspense over a truffle: only in the Dordogne.

* * * * * *

Sweet moments, when I realized that I was truly learning French:

- Being able to read and understand all of the graffiti in a public restroom— even the slang for body parts. I often received annoyed looks from the women who were waiting to use the toilet. I'm sure they had no idea how much enjoyment I had gotten from reading all the writing on the walls, but they saw me exit the stall looking very pleased with myself.

- Automatically saying "bless you" in French at the hair salon when my stylist sneezed (all seven people in the salon stopped what they were doing, turned to look at me, and said, "Ahhh," with big smiles on their faces).

- Being confident enough to answer the phone without worrying about the upcoming blind French conversation. (I still made a lot of errors but have decided not to be afraid of the telephone.)

- Going to the local bar to pick up a delivery they were holding for me, when the bartender heard me ask, "Hello, do you have a drink for me?" instead of "Hello, do you have a box for me?" I explained in French that the courier had told me to come to the bar for the box, because he couldn't find my house. The seven men sitting on the barstools were enjoying the "show" the bartender and I put on, and one gave me permission to speak in English. Here was the sweet moment: without even thinking, I said, "No thank you, I only want to speak French." One man clapped, one raised his glass to me, and they all cheered.

- Being able to successfully avoid French bureaucracy. The Domme hospital/senior rest home director had asked me to write a formal request explaining why I would like to visit with healthy, long-term residents, when I had stopped in one day to ask if visits would be possible. I realized it would be easier just to visit with those residents who were sitting outside the center to smoke. I always asked the person first if he or she would like to chat. Every single time, a big smile came to the person's face, and a couple of times, the cigarette was put out to allow the patient to fully concentrate on my French. I asked open-ended questions, so I could hear their long answers. The senior got the chance to share cherished memories with an interested person, and I got a lovely French conversation. It was a win/win situation.

* * * * * *

Finally the long awaited day of the truffle hunt arrived. I expected to see everyone at Jean-Paul's, but when I arrived, Jean-Paul was alone and he led me to his car.

"This just came back from the garage, so let us see what it can do," he said. "We will look at some of the fields on the way to my friend's house. Some of these farmers know what they're doing and others, well…"

I quickly fastened my safety belt. My granddad was a farmer who liked reviewing crops, and often, when he was the driver, he would focus more on his neighbor's farming techniques and less on the current, unimportant task of driving. Like my granddad, Jean-Paul liked to point, and he offered a running commentary, but his driving was very safe.

"That is a good-looking walnut orchard, but he should trim those dead limbs. Now this guy over here doesn't know what he is doing." His comments that made me feel like I was back riding with my granddad.

We traveled down the valley and over the hill to another very small community. His friend's farm overlooked the valley with a spectacular view where the healthy shade trees didn't block it. A low stone wall with moss here and there circled the house. Traditional faded-blue shutters hung at the windows. The superstar dog, a black and white Australian collie, was the first one to greet us at the gate. He barked, but he wagged his tail. Monsieur walked out of the front door of a traditional rural farmhouse, where the barn is connected to the house. He put on his hat, patted the dog on the head to thank him for doing his job, and opened the gate to join us as we got out of the car.

"We are here," Jean-Paul stated.

"Let's go to my 'office.' Follow me."

All of us carefully walked through the huge weed-free garden as we made our way to the rustic barn door.

"Just wait here. I'll be right back. This morning I went out and found some beauties for you."

"So you didn't steal them from your neighbor's spot?" Jean-Paul teased.

"I stepped over those sad morsels on my way to my secret place. That young kid thinks he has found a goldmine, and I suppose there is some poor fool out there who will buy them."

Monsieur disappeared into the barn with the dog at his heels. We didn't wait long until they returned. He had a small green basket in his hand, filled with truffles. The earthy smell rose up to my nose.

"Those are beauties," Jean-Paul told him.

"Some of them are good enough for a Californian, I think. Have you eaten truffles before?" he asked me.

"No, this is my first time."

"Well, they have a very strong taste, so only use a small amount. Also, don't wash them, because water will destroy them and they are too precious to waste." He handed the basket to Jean-Paul to hold so he could select some of the large, dark truffles. "Hold out your hands," he told me.

I held out both hands cupped together in order to hold those expensive treasures. The worst thing I could do was drop one of these rare delicacies. Monsieur slowly turned each truffle around in front of his face, inspecting it before putting it in my hands. I didn't expect him to give me so many, but seven truffles passed his inspection to end up in my hands.

"Do you see the markings on this one?" Jean-Paul asked me. "This is where a wild pig started to eat it. You know it is a good one when a pig wants it."

"Come in the house and say hello to the wife," Monsieur said.

As we walked back to the house, they told me about training the dog to hunt for truffles.

"This dog is very smart. I started training him about truffles when he was just a young puppy. His nose is better than a pig's, and he won't eat the truffle."

"You feed him bacon as a reward for finding a truffle, don't you?" Jean-Paul asked.

"There is a certain justice in using pork," his friend replied.

We climbed the stone steps and entered the house straight into the kitchen. A truly magnificent French sight greeted us. *Foie gras* and *paté* were being made that day. The long wooden table in the

53

center of the room was covered with tidy, butchered ducks and geese. The tools that had been used to cut the carcasses had been cleaned and were now lined up along one side of the table. No feathers or blood were in sight. The meaty body parts were grouped together. All the carcasses were stacked eight high, all the hearts were piled together, and the most important organs of the delicacy, the livers, were in a pan of water to preserve them until it was cooking time. All the parts of the bird were put to good use either in the *foie gras* or as part of the dinner. Even the meat on the neck was saved, thus confirming that nothing was wasted. The mastermind of the operation was a short, grey-haired woman, who wore a clean, striped apron over a floral dress. Her hair was tied back in a bun, with not a hair out of place, even though she had just butchered eight birds.

"Oh, Jean-Paul, now you'll know what you and Colette will be getting for Christmas," madame said after the introductions.

"I always look forward to your *foie gras*."

"This looks like a lot of work. May I take pictures?" I asked.

"Of course, but I am a mess. What you see here is the way my mother taught me how to make *foie gras*. It takes all day, but it is worth it for the taste."

Jean-Paul nodded his head in agreement.

Madame explained detailed cooking techniques to me, I assumed. Unfortunately I couldn't understand her advice and cooking secrets. There was some Occitan mixed in with her French, but mostly the lost conversation was due to my poor French. It was time to return to Cénac et St. Julien, so we said our good-byes and thank you's. Once I returned home, I shared two truffles with Claire. Then I ate truffle omelettes for dinner every evening for two weeks. It was heaven.

* * * * * * *

So many aspects and nuances of the French language were completely unknown to me. I learned things that were never mentioned in my high school classes. The list would be too long to include all of them, but a few of the interesting ones were:

- The sound of any verb conjugated in the first person for the future "I will" and the conditional "I would" is exactly the same, but they are spelled differently. The listener has to hear the whole sentence to understand if the speaker means "I will" or "I would."

- One little accent can make two exact words mean different things. For example, the word for wall and ripe are the same, mur and mûr—except for an accent used on ripe. Or, the verb for fish and peach; pêche, is the same as to sin: péché. The only difference is the accents.

- Words can be spelled the same, but have different meanings because of their gender. *Le vase* is a vase for flowers, but *la vase* is slime or mud. Another favorite example is le mari means husband, but la mari is marijuana.

- The French do not use contractions like don't, can't, I'm in their writing.

- Homonyms are found in English and in French. The French word for liver, faith, time, and a city in Southern France all sound the same. Likewise the word for blood, without, and hundred sound the same, but are not spelled alike.

- French has reflective verbs meaning verbs where an action is done to one's self. Some are easy to understand like to brush your teeth, to introduce yourself, or to sit down. Others are more complicated to grasp, but the rule of thumb is if feelings are involved then the sentence is reflective. So 'I had a good time' or 'you got angry' or 'the door slammed shut' are reflective sentences. The same sentences in English would literally mean 'I me had a good time', 'you you got angry', and 'the door it slammed shut.'

* * * * * *

"Now I'm going to teach you what you really need to know, but for some fucking reason, teachers in school don't tell you," Emma announced at the beginning of class.

"First off, you may have noticed that I never swear in French. It just isn't satisfying, and most French people prefer to swear in English. If it's a situation that demands a proper 'f' you, then say 'fuck you.'"

"But will the French understand me?" I asked, even though I knew I would never say it to a French person.

"Oh, they will understand you and respect you for it."

"I don't think I would say that, because it might start something I know I couldn't finish, and because, well, I've never said it. Ever," Hazel said.

"Really Hazel? You never swear, even when you're angry?" the curious part of me had to know.

"Oh no, never. One time I did say, 'Sugar!' but I don't think that counts."

Emma stood up by the white board and started writing.

"Okay, you know those times when you're driving down the tight, narrow lanes, trying to get on with your life and there, standing in the middle of the fucking road, is a group of people, most likely tourists. They see you coming, but they just stand there anyway. You patiently wait for them to move—they don't. They just keep looking at a stone building like they've never seen a stone building in their life. You want to yell at them, 'Just walk down any fucking lane in France, and you will see a stone building. Get out of my way!'"

"I don't think I know how to say all of that. Plus I'd get it wrong, so they would come closer to my car to figure out what I'm saying," Sue said.

"All you need to know for those situations, and believe me, you will need to know this because the summer tourist season is coming, is to yell 'Ras-le-bol!' That means 'Fed up!' Every French person has said it at one time or another. They will move. Or you could yell 'Franchement!' This means 'Honestly!'"

"Is it rude?" Hazel asked.

"No, it's perfectly acceptable and it will work. People, even those struck dumb by a common stone building, will move. Now another phrase that will be useful is 'Je m'en fous.' You might want to memorize that. It means 'I don't give a damn.' Or if a person is telling you an outrageous story ending with a stupid suggestion involving you, you could say '*Ca va pas, la tête*!' This means 'Are you off your head?' The unsaid part of that question is that there is no fucking way I would do something that stupid."

"This is good stuff." I said, writing like mad.

"It's the perfect thing to say when you're furious at the fool who's talking, probably non-stop. Another very important thing is you want to sound like an intelligent person when talking about money, especially when buying something. '*Combien coûte-il?*' means 'How much does it cost?' And if you ask a stranger for help, have manners. Start the conversation with '*Un renseignement, si vous plaît?*' It's like asking, 'Do you have a minute, please?' because the unspoken, implied part of the question is I need to ask you a million questions about this strange, wonderful French way."

"People in France have been so kind to me. Never have I run into anyone who is rude. I don't know why some Americans have bad impressions of the French," I said.

"That's because you have manners, Karen, and the French value manners," Emma said.

"They really should teach these things in a regular class," Sue said.

"Well, this is not your mother's French class!"

"I'll drink to that. Time to open the wine!"

* * * * * * *

At the Cénac et St. Julien weekly outdoor market, we had a favorite rôtisserie truck, which sold delicious, slow-roasted chickens, pigeons, quail, pork ribs, and ham. An additional reason to shop there was the friendly owner, Eric, a slim, tall man in his forties, who always had a huge smile on his face. No matter how long the line of customers was, he always took the time to welcome and banter with his guests. Most were long-time regulars with their favorite orders already known to Eric. Eric treated me with the same acceptance as his regulars, and I enjoyed all my conversations with him as well as the tasty chicken dinners. One exchange stands out as memorable. It all started (of course after the customary polite greetings were exchanged) when I asked about MSG. My parents were visiting us for two weeks and my eighty-eight year old father had special dietary requirements.

"It looks great, but my Dad cannot eat meat with MSG on it. It makes his stomach very sick. Does your meat have MSG?" I asked.

"What is MSG?" he asked. His lack of knowledge was a good sign; however, I needed to make sure it was safe for my Dad. I couldn't remember the word for food, but that didn't stop me.

"MSG is put on meat to make it fresh for a long time. It is a preservative."

"It is a preservative," he slowly repeated.

"Yes, it is a preservative that makes my Dad sick."

"Are you sure? Oh, I think what you mean is an additive."

"Well, yes. They are the same thing."

By this time his three assistants in the truck had huge smiles and could barely keep from laughing. The twenty people who were waiting in line had gathered closer to catch every word—after all this was a free show while waiting for their chickens.

"Well, noooo, they are not the same thing." He leaned in closer to me in order to quietly school me. "A preservative is a condom," he said with a twinkle in his eye. My roar of laughter mingled with everyone else's. All the business in the truck paused so everyone could enjoy this useful vocabulary lesson. A French lesson and shopping for dinner all at the same time: that was time management.

Non Karen, On se Tutoie Maintenant

(No Karen, We Use 'Tu' With Each Other Now)

Two tickets to the 31st *Exposition Nationale d'Aviculture* were leaning against our front door several weeks later when we returned from our town's outdoor market. Claire must have dropped them off, fulfilling her promise. This Saturday she would be showing her pigeons, hoping for another champion. I really wanted to ask her how she prepared her birds for the judges. Did she blow-dry their feathers or try to train them to stretch out their wings in order to show off their colors and wingspan? But I didn't ask, because my French might lead her to think I was asking about how to cook them again.

The expo was held in Souillac, a town of about 4,000, known for its 12th century abbey and Roman architecture. It also has a respected culinary school. Again, I made a note to myself not to mention the cooking school to Claire, since edible champion birds and rabbits would be surrounded us.

While trying to find the hall, we became hopelessly lost. On the bright side, it allowed me to see new areas of the village and to talk to strangers, while asking for directions. People were surprised to have a Californian standing before them, but they were even more shocked by my intent to find a bird show.

"A bird show? That is not a typical tourist activity," one man said.

"I like to think of myself as a local. I am here for a year, but I wish my time in France was longer. I want to be as French as I can."

"We need more visitors like you. Okay, I think I know the hall you seek."

As we made our way to the hall, my helper's comment triggered a memory of another conversation I had had in English and French with a couple from Paris who were dining at the table next to mine about a month before. I had explained my situation and goal, and they were wistful. The man explained the indifference he found at his job.

"I teach beginning and intermediate level French to immigrants at a night school, and it is extremely rare to find a student who wants to assimilate into the French society. All of them are uninterested in the French way of life. I applaud you for learning about other cultures than your own. But honestly, if someone moves to another country, you'd think that person would want to be part of his new, adopted home."

By the time we found the hall and parked, the expo was in full progress. The entry lobby was filled with exhibitors taking a break between showings. The refreshment stand was in the far corner, filling the lobby with sweet smells of freshly made chocolate crêpes, coffee, and wine.

Three men wearing berets stood at the main doors collecting tickets and they were pleasantly surprised to hear our accents.

"Oh, you are from California? This is a first for us. Welcome! We have the California quail in the show that you might enjoy and many other birds."

I was impressed and whispered to Steve.

"Man, he knew our state bird. I don't know the national bird of France."

"It's the rooster," my husband said.

"Oh yeah. How did you know that?"

"It was on the national rugby team's jerseys, remember?"

The second we entered the main hall we were blasted by the noise. The twenty-five long tables of caged chickens, roosters, pigeons, quail, peacocks, ducks, guineas, and pheasants must have had something to complain about at a cranked, surround-sound, stereo-quality volume. It was a cacophony of bird sounds. I appreciated the silent bunnies more and more. But once we

became accustomed to the noise level, not to mention the smell, we were able to enjoy the beauty of the birds. The birds were grouped by type. Blue and red ribbons hung on some of the cages, and certificates hung from others. The morning judging had already taken place, but the grand champions had yet to be announced. Historically, the French view pigeons, especially homing pigeons, with great respect. During World War I, a homing pigeon named Cher Ami carried twelve important messages across dangerous territory, saving many French lives. This earned her the prestigious *Croix de Guerre* award. The resistance force in World War II regularly used homing pigeons, because radio communication was too risky, and the pigeons played a critical role in the successful Invasion of Normandy.

"You are here!" Claire said.

Claire kissed Steve and I, and then Claire brought us up to date.

"It was a very close judging this morning, very stressful. My Coco and Edith were confident and beautiful, but the competition was fierce."

"Oooh, I would like to see your birds. Where are they?"

"This way, I will show you."

Claire had a huge smile and a bounce in her step. She led us to a cage with two bright blue ribbons on it, and a smug, fat pigeon sitting in the corner. In the next cage, Coco had won two blue ribbons of her own, and she looked even more proud of herself than Edith.

"Claire, congratulations!"

"This means both of my girls go on to the grand championship judging later today."

"Good luck."

Claire was called away, so we headed over to the rabbit section. Extremely fat, extremely adorable bunnies sat in their cages nibbling on various snacks. It's said that 93% of the rabbit can be used in some commercial manner or other, but their cuteness kept me from thinking of them as anything other than soft, fuzzy pets.

"Karen and Steve, quickly come with me. The final judging is about to start. Ignore those silly rabbits."

Claire led the way, dodging through the crowd, to reach the stage at the back of the room. Six cages were arranged in a line on a table and four judges examined the first pigeon. Coco was to be the second one judged. Of course I only knew that because Claire recognized her beloved bird and told me. Claire was nervous. Her eyes followed the judges' every move as they inspected the first bird's feathers, head, and feet, and she softly mumbled to herself giving her own opinions. I heard her evaluation of the first bird though, and it was tough. Claire had high standards. I wasn't sure if I should interrupt her thoughts during the judging, but she turned to me.

"You know, I love my pigeons. Growing up in a big family and living in Paris was hard. We didn't have anything. The only pet I ever had was an injured pigeon that I found on our windowsill and I cared for her. She grew to trust me. I would sing to her—silly, I know."

"No, that is sweet."

"My mother liked my pigeon too, as long as I cleaned any mess that she made. Pigeons bring good memories to me."

The judges moved to Coco's cage and one reached in to bring the calm bird out. They inspected her as carefully as the other bird, made notes, and then they moved on to the next bird.

"I think they liked her," I said.

"We will see. There is always Edith too. She is the last one."

I mentally wondered how she recognized her pigeons from so far away.

The wait for the announcement of the grand champion took about an hour once all the birds were evaluated. Claire visited with friends from the association while we ate a *crêpe*. Finally, the lead judge called for everyone's attention. The big moment had arrived.

"Ladies and gentlemen, we are pleased to announce this year's champion. But first I must say that all the birds were exceptional, and all the owners should be proud. It was a difficult decision."

I scanned the crowd and found Claire intently staring at the announcer, her hands clasped together.

"The 2014 grand champion is ..."

Like every game show announcer who knew how to milk a moment, he paused to build the suspense.

".....the beautiful Edith, owned by Claire."

People were clapping, Henri shyly kissed Claire's cheek, and then she made her way up on the stage to receive the trophy. I was so happy for her.

While standing in line at my *boulangerie,* waiting for my turn, I noticed a small handwritten note taped to the cash register. The annual two-week-long spring school holidays were just around the corner, and one enterprising young pre-teen had put up a sign advertising his babysitting services. I'm less work than a baby, I thought. And if he is already trained at figuring out what a non-communicative person is trying to express, then he might be the tutor for me. Before I got around to calling, I was reading the want ads in the local newspaper, and I noticed another interesting ad. In this one, a young professional woman had a few hours per week available to babysit children to supplement her salary. This was the universe telling me it was time to act on securing a tutor. I put down the newspaper and picked up my phone.

"Hello. Is this the person who wants to watch children?" I asked.

"Eh, yes, I am. I'm Marie."

"I don't have children, but can you help me?" With limited language, I had to get right to the point.

"I don't know," she cautiously said. "What do you need help with?"

"Well, my French is bad, and I need a teacher to work with me."

"Oh, French lessons. Sure, I can help you."

We worked out a weekly schedule of class times and meeting places. When I met Marie the following Monday evening, I had a long list of French grammar questions. Marie arrived with props as well. She was prepared with French books, exercises that were far too difficult, and French games. Not only did she patiently answer my grammar questions and repeatedly do the French numbers drill so I could become more comfortable with them, but she also tutored me in French slang. Sometimes it was slang I would never need, but it was interesting to learn.

My slang lesson came about because of an email I had written. Marie and I exchanged emails to arrange our meetings, and we always wrote in French. Then at the beginning of the next lesson, she would review my email's grammatical errors. I had written what I thought was a standard polite phrase, "Thank you, I look forward to our next meeting." At our next class, Marie kept her eyes down and quietly laid my email on the table between us. She seemed a bit uncomfortable. We happened to be meeting in a crowded, noisy café, but she spoke in a low voice.

"I am not too sure how to explain this. We would not say this to each other," she said, pointing to my comment. "Please tell me in English what you mean."

I told her and then asked what it meant to her.

"Well, technically your use of the verb is correct; however, this verb's meaning has changed in modern times. Now couples only use this verb to say thank you for the satisfying sex," she said with a pink face.

"YOU HAVE A VERB FOR THAT?" I managed to say, roaring with laughter. I couldn't resist but had to clarify. "You have a verb for thank you for a climax?"

By this time Marie was laughing too. "Yes, we do. We talk about everything."

Needless to say, I was careful not to casually use that verb again. Sometimes the important lesson is to learn what not to say.

* * * * * * *

As much as I enjoyed exploring other places in France, I loved coming back to Cénac et St. Julien. It was true what they said: the people make the place. Nothing made me feel more like I belonged than running into people I knew. At the outdoor market, I saw Chef from the bakery, still wearing his apron along with a little flour dust on his sleeves. His dark, black eyes were sharp as always, even at this "late hour" for him.

"I thought you would be sleeping now," I joked with him, since it was 11 a.m.

"Oh la, la, yesterday I slept for 11 hours, so I am good today," he said.

Before leaving on one of my short trips, I had dropped off copies of the photos I took when watching him make bread. I asked if he had found the pictures, because he might have missed them in all the activity at the bakery.

"Karen, yes, the pictures are wonderful. I liked them so much that they are on my Facebook page. Thank you," he said.

After a promise to check out his page, I noticed another friend who owned the Press in town. We kissed hello, and as we exchanged news, I noticed a small group of tourists walking by, looking confused and exhausted. My first thought was, "That could be me. I am so lucky. This connection I made is so special."

Now all this inner perspective was going on as the French conversation was still taking place, and I should have been focusing on the French. After a week and a half of being away from French, my brain felt like a muscle I hadn't used in a while. Having to think about every word I wanted to say was as heavy as the French dictionary I carried. It wasn't until I'd had a break from my routine by taking a short trip to England that I realized how stressful it was to learn another language.

One day I was assigned homework from Eric, the owner of the rôtisserie truck found at our weekly outdoor market. As I waited in the customary long line of customers, Eric and his assistants caught sight of me towards the end of the line and yelled their hellos. When it was my turn at the counter, I asked Eric's wife, Sophie how her week had been, which she answered by describing her canoe adventures.

"It was like cowboys and Indians," she told me.

"You needed John Wayne with you," I said.

"No," Eric said, as he removed his hat. "I am more like Yul Brynner." His shaved, bald head confirmed his observation.

I thought of another tough guy, so I added, "Or Clint Eastwood – he is a good cowboy. Do you know him? He said 'Make my day.'"

Eric looked confused. "Do you mean 'Have a nice day?'"

"Oh no. Clint was never nice." I made a gun using my fingers to look more in character with Dirty Harry. "He was only difficult (I couldn't think of how to say mean or threatening), and he said 'Make my day.'"

"Karen, you must explain this to us next week. Who is this cowboy and why does he wish people a good day and then kill them? That is strange."

This was a cultural misunderstanding, partially due to my mixing up Clint Eastwood's film characters. The following week, I arrived at Eric's truck with two photographs of Clint Eastwood: one as Dirty Harry and another of him as a drifter in a Western. I believed they would help him understand. Also I had studied my dictionary and now I knew the verb "to threaten" and how to say "it would make me happy to kill you" in French. I never thought I would need that sentence in ANY language! After buying my dinner *caille* (quail), Eric and I had a quick lesson. Once he saw the Dirty Harry picture, he recognized the movie character. I didn't ever need to speak my horrible threat, but I had it in my bank of knowledge.

* * * * * *

Americans share a lot of holidays with the French: New Year's Eve, Easter, Veteran's Day, Christmas, to name just a few. I enjoyed all the French holidays, but some had an unusual historical aspect or a particularly colorful manner in how the French celebrated the holidays that intrigued me. Here were some of my favorites:

> *Carnival*

As in many places around the world, *Carnival* is a festive season, which occurs before Lent. Limoux, in the Aude region, hosts one of the oldest celebrations in France and has the longest carnival season in the world. It is often characterized by a colorful, sometimes wild, parade of masked, costumed people. The typical costume is called the *pierrot*. It is usually a silk baggy tunic and pantaloon resembling a pajama-like outfit, always completed with white gloves, a matching hat, and a mask that covers the entire face. The bold print and colors belong to the same guild so the same costume will remain in a family for generations. If a masked dancer taps you on the head with the long reed called the *carabène*, it means he or she knows you. The band that accompanies the dancers plays the same haunting tune over and over, while the dancers usually have their hands in the air, striking a pose on the beat. Confetti is very generously thrown by the handful from the dancers and is an important part of the festival, forming a connection between the

dancers and the spectators. After the parade passes, the ground looks like it snowed. Twelve years before I had witnessed Limoux's carnival, and the only difference from the present day event is that the dancers no longer distributed free glasses of the local sparkling wine, Blanquette de Limoux, to the spectators (even to the children). The delicious wine is still available, but only for a nominal fee at the wine tent.

Cénac et St. Julien had a Saturday morning parade with confetti, masked people, and costumed children with decorated bicycles as the main component of the parade. There was also a ceremony during school hours, which I was lucky enough to witness. The costumed elementary school children, along with their teachers and some members of the community, gathered at the village square for a mock trial. Seven children lined up in front, waiting to read their script, while behind them a scarecrow was tied to a pole embedded in a pile of kindling and small wood. The scarecrow was always called Pétassou, the accused, who was believed to be responsible for all

the bad things that happened that year. Each of the seven children read a grievance against Pétassou, and the crowd reacted with boos and oooh, la, la's. When the last crime was read, and the children had wasted no time in reaching their guilty verdict, a seven year old walked over to the nine year old who held a can of gasoline. Oh no! Children with gasoline and matches, I thought. This can't be happening. The parents and teachers around me were smiling and having a good time.

"The children make a fire?" I asked a stranger standing next to me.

"Yes. It is a tradition. But don't worry, the teacher is close by," she said.

The nine-year-old had a great time thoroughly dousing Pétassou with gasoline, and the seven year old lit and threw the rag at Pétassou's feet. It was a rapid, substantial fire. Everyone stepped back from the blaze and enjoyed the heat at Pétassou's expense.

> April 1st or *Le Poisson d'Avril (April's Fish)*
> There is one main prank played on this day: secretly attaching a paper fish to the back of an unsuspecting person. It's not completely clear how this tradition started. The common beliefs about that are since fishing is forbidden at this time of year, it's funny to give a fake fish, or, because it is close to Easter, when fish is commonly eaten, then it is appropriate to give a "fish." Also on this day, the television news and the newspapers will announce a false, outrageous story. The next day they will issue a retraction. On April 1st when I read that chickens in the region have perfected how to lay a square egg, I knew I found the joke on the front page.

➤ Mother's Day or *Fête des Mères*

This holiday began in France as early as 1806. In 1929, the French government recognized the day in order to honor only the mothers of large families. In 1941, Marshal Philippe Pétain, under the Vichy government, placed the holiday on the national calendar as part of a campaign to encourage population growth, and all mothers were honored.

➤ Music Day or Fête de la Musique

The first Music Day was held in 1982 in France and has since spread to over 32 countries. In the U.S., it is celebrated in Massachusetts, California, New York City, and Chicago. The purpose of the festival is to celebrate and encourage all kinds of music; therefore, on June 21st, free public performances by professional and amateur musicians are performed in the streets, on outdoor stages, and in halls. In France, it is estimated that each year 10 million people take to the streets to attend a musical event.

My village was part of the national *Fête de la Musique* as well. Together, Cénac et St. Julien and Domme offered an evening outdoor performance of folk and rock & roll bands in Domme's public park. Emma's band played that night and was a local favorite. Her three person band consisted of a drummer and a guitarist who also were the back-up singers, and Emma who was the lead singer. Sometimes she hit a tambourine against her hip as she sang classic French songs and a few ones in English as well. The first time I heard her sing was in December at a charity event in Domme and the tone of her voice reminded me of Marianne Faithful. Every time I saw Emma on stage she wore her favorite, good-luck-charm, sunflower print long dress when she performed and this night was no different. Emma joked with the audience between songs and acknowledged friends, but she never swore on stage. People were invited to dance or sit on the grass under the stars. Some families brought their own refreshments, and others enjoyed the snacks, wine, and killer-strong punch served at the community booth. A unique aspect of our fête was the bonfire. We combined the bonfire associated with Saint Jean Baptiste Day, which is on June 24th, with our Music Day. The bonfire had pagan roots to celebrate the summer solstice. When Christianity came to France, the celebration shifted to honor the birth of John the Baptist.

The bonfire was the symbol of light in both senses: one for the sun and the other for John the Baptist, who brought the Light of the Message to Christians.

Domme was lucky to have a sculptor as a resident who always made the burnable art piece and the shape of our sculpted wood bonfire changed each year. That year's shape was a jeep, in tribute to a recently deceased pillar of the community. He had been the leader in the preservation of the medieval stone walls that circled the village, and his jeep had often been sighted out by the ramparts.

➢ Beaujolais Nouveau Day

How fitting that there is a wine holiday in France, a country that loves its wine! The third Thursday in November is the traditional day of tasting the new wine. It is a light, fruity, red wine, fermented and aged only 6 to 8 weeks instead of the usual months or years of other red wines. Each year, 70 million bottles are consumed worldwide. I did my part for the 2014 statistic.

* * * * * * *

"My mother would never let us play this game," Jean-Paul told me, shaking his head at the crazy thought. "My sisters and I would have gotten in trouble if we mistreated our geese."

"They were not a toy," I said.

"No, they were important as food, only as food. They were not considered as pets either, like how the British treat their farm animals." Again he shook his head in bewilderment.

73

Jean-Paul and I were standing by the fence at the geese pen at the *La Ringueta Fête* in Sarlat. It was a two-day festival of music, food, and games, which celebrated the Occitan language and the historical way of life. This particular game involved tossing a ring on a goose's long neck to win. The geese were not too crazy about the game, and they did their best to avoid the ring. They were panting and had a wild-eyed look as they huddled close together.

Old French, or the dialect of Occitan, was undergoing a resurgence of popularity and was now being valued as part of this region's heritage. The renewed interest was evident as elementary and middle schools offered immersion programs; universities offered classes in Occitan; local television channels broadcast programs in Occitan; and the regional newspaper had a weekly column in Occitan. Occitan is the historical tongue of southern France, related to Catalan, and was a major medieval language. It was the language of choice for the troubadours. However, in northern France, Latin-based French held the prestige and power. In 1539, a royal decree proclaimed French the official language. Then the *Academie Francaise* was founded in 1637, with the aim to safeguard the standard language and keep it as pure as possible. Regional dialects became known as "*patois,*" a derogatory term for the unofficial languages or dialects. During the French Revolution in the late 18th century, it was considered unpatriotic to speak anything other than French. Towards the end of the revolution, Abbé Grégoire presented a report to the National Convention on the need and means to extirpate the *patois* languages, even though only one tenth of the population at that time was fluent in French.

The government's systematic approach to killing the *patois* took root in the educational system. *La Vergonha* (meaning "The Shame") is what the people called the effects of the vicious policies aimed at their children, causing them to reject, to feel ashamed of, or humiliated by their native tongue. The 1851 French Teaching Law stated, "It is strictly forbidden to speak *patois* during classes or break." And what happened to the child if caught speaking her or his first language at school? Sometimes the child was hit, or was made to kneel on a ruler under a large sign, which said "Speak French and Be Clean." Often the "troublemaker" was made to hold a log or wear a heavy clog around the neck for as long as necessary, until another child spoke Occitan and the punishment was passed to him. Sometimes the punishment lasted as long as several days. Even if the teacher did not hear the offensive language personally, the children were encouraged to inform on each other.

Thankfully, Occitan was not lost even though it came close in 1993, when the fluency rate dropped to less than 7%. I was incredibly lucky to become friends with native Occitan speakers, and even more so to be at the Sarlat festival with one. When I asked Jean-Paul to join me, he had been pleased.

"Jean-Paul, you can tell me if the childhood games are true."

"What I remember of my childhood is work, not games, but I will go. It may be cultural for you *and* me. I will learn what the other children were playing," he said with a smile.

"Did you play any games?"

"I wanted to play rugby, but my father said I was too small, so I played football," which the Americans call soccer.

The spacious, tree-covered parking lot in Sarlat was cleared for the small center stage, food booths, and game spaces. The public was invited to step back in time and play the rural games of days gone by. The space hosting the forerunner of the game of *pétanque* was popular and very similar to the present day game: throwing balls as close as possible to a smaller metal ball called the *cochonnet,* (which means piglet) for points. The local flavor influenced several games, such as trying to crack a walnut shot out of a hollow log, or the aforementioned goose game. Games of skill and balance were prevalent too; like challenging a person to stay on a greased, moving log while sitting on a barrel, or trying to climb a greased pole to grab a flag.

But I think the part of the festival that Jean-Paul enjoyed the most was listening to the local elementary children sing folk songs in Occitan on the center stage. The four-, five-, and six-year-olds, dressed in the traditional costume of white lace collar shirts with red bandanas tied around their necks and black pants, or long black skirts, sang loudly and proudly. Jean-Paul's lips silently moved along with their words, and he swayed slightly with the music. Maybe good memories were happening for him. I hoped so.

No French festival would be complete without great food. The strong tempting smell of garlic announced a tasty meal. Three large boars slowly rotated on a spit over glowing red charcoals, their heads and feet still attached. Men in berets brushed oil and herbs on the pigs and wiped the sweat off their brows, their glasses of wine and cigarettes never far from their workstation. Other men stirred the three 40-gallon wok-shaped pots of cooked garlic and simmering rice in broth.

"Would you like to play a game before we leave?" I asked Jean-Paul.

"It is you who must play a game. Let's try *pétanque*. I will teach you."

* * * * * * *

"Excuse me, do you have more swimsuits?" I asked the young sales assistant. I was in a sports store in Sarlat, and there was a wall covered in suits in many colors and styles. They all appeared to be two-piece swimsuits though.

"I will help you find a suit for your body," the sales assistant offered. She critically looked me up and down, which is awful at most times, but really dreadful when being mentally measured for a swimsuit.

"Here is a good one, and I hear you are British, so I give you the two pieces."

"Oh no, I want a one-piece," I said. She had no idea that she was talking to a shy person who has never worn a two-piece swimsuit in public in her whole life.

The sales assistant's eyebrows shot up. "Okay, good for you," she said, as she put the top piece of the swimsuit back on the wall.

"Oh, no, no, no. I want a one-piece."

"Yes, you have a one-piece."

She and I were clearly caught in a cultural misunderstanding.

"I need a one-piece for all this." I used my hand in a circle motion from shoulders to hips and felt like a diva on a bad reality TV show. What a time to forget the word for body.

"Oh, you want a swimsuit for an older woman? You are too young and pretty. They are over here. Follow me."

She walked me over to the corner and left me in peace to browse. I'd found a cute swimsuit, a French conversation, and a welcome compliment all in the same swimsuit department. That was a pretty good day.

During the drive home, the car alarm started dinging. Then the oil light on the dashboard lit up. What now? I was already stressed from trying on swimsuits; I couldn't take much more. Immediately, I mentally reviewed French car vocabulary, while at the same time reproaching myself for leaving my French dictionary at home. I slowed down and decided to continue the short distance to my favorite gas station. I traveled so slowly that the farm tractors and bicycles passed me. At the gas station, the mechanic couldn't find what was wrong and he checked the oil supply to confirm that it was full. "Cars are delicate and complicated things. You probably should go to the dealer in Sarlat," he told me.

Off I went, retracing my route back to Sarlat, only this time I turned up the volume of the radio to drown out the car alarm. As I listened to the radio personality explain how to cook pigeon, I realized something important. My purse, filled with my French books, large camera, walking shoes, English book, wallet, and other important stuff was sitting in the passenger seat, and it weighed a ton. I carefully reached over to place my purse on the car floor to be rewarded with a silenced alarm and only the sound of the radio voice saying, "*Voilà*." That was a perfectly timed coincidence. The car had wanted my purse in the passenger seat to wear a safety belt. By this time, I was very close to the car dealer, and since I didn't want to miss a language opportunity, I pulled into the garage. The attendant may have been good at fixing cars, I didn't know. I did know he was the perfect language partner. He only spoke French, and if I didn't understand something then he explained it a different way, and he spoke slowly. On one hand I felt guilty for taking his time, but on the other I felt very happy with the technical conversation we had.

No sounds are more representative of summertime than the sputter of the sprinkler watering the garden and the purr of a lawnmower. Steve and I were relaxing on the gravel terrace under the persimmon tree, after a hot day of sightseeing with the sound of Henri's lawnmower engine in the background. We sipped our glasses of white wine and read, each in our own preferred language. The wisteria beside our table twisted along the iron railing, with dashes of purple dotted here and there, but the view of green hills was still open. The lower portion of our yard was a grassy area with a picnic table. We preferred the higher terrace because of its shaded, cozy space, which was also closer to the house for when we happened to be carrying out a tray of food.

Suddenly there was an abrupt span of silence, and we looked over the railing to check on Henri.

"It looks beautiful, Henri. Come have a glass of wine or something cold to drink with us," I shouted down to him.

"That would be good. Thank you."

From around the corner, where Henri's and our lower properties met and their clothesline stood, Claire poked her head out from the hung, washed clothes.

"Oh, Claire, can you join us for a cold drink too?"

When everyone was settled around our little, square wooden table with glasses filled, we toasted to friends around the world.

"There was a time when we had a big vegetable and flower garden in this grassy area below us," Claire said.

"That was with the previous owner. She was a nice, older widow who didn't use the space, so she let us use it. We always shared the vegetables with her," Henri said.

"I don't think she was able to work in a garden at her age, and the price of food is so expensive. It is important to have a garden all year long. Well, you know the prices. Do you think it is expensive?" Claire asked.

"All the food is more expensive here. We find that things are twice the price they are in California. Only wine is a good price—except the very famous labels. And I never knew that cheese was so expensive, but then I never knew there were so many flavors of cheese," I said. At the time I couldn't think of how to say "kinds of cheese," but flavors worked.

"Living in the countryside helps with the cost of food. We have gardens, we preserve, and we hunt."

Henri interrupted, "Hunt for mushrooms, nuts, and for greens. Hunting is not just for meat."

"Some people have chickens, ducks, and geese for eggs and meat," Claire said.

"And for awards too," I said, with a knowing smile.

Claire laughed. "Only the most beautiful have awards."

"Do you miss going to all the specialty shops? You know, the French traditional way: one for cheese, one for meat, one for vegetables?"

"I grew up in Paris, and all the little shops were available to us. We certainly didn't have a garden. It was just the way to shop; each place sold what they did best, and we didn't think anything of it. I remember when very big, American style grocery stores opened."

"That was in the early 60s, I think," Henri said.

"Yes, I think you're right. For me, having young children, it was a good thing. It was so much easier shopping in one place, and the selection was much larger than what we were used to."

Glasses were refilled and we settled in to enjoy the leisurely early evening hours of milder sunlight, when the temperatures dropped.

"It is just a little sad to lose the French traditional way. I have a difficult time finding a cheese shop," I said.

"It is difficult for the small shops to compete against the big ones. It's true. I know a good one in Sarlat and in Perigueux. Tell me the next time you are going to those cities, and I will give you the addresses," Claire said.

"Did the owner of the house tell you about the stone wall that is below us?" Henri asked.

"No, he didn't say a thing. Why?"

"Last year, after heavy rains, this stone wall completely collapsed," he said.

"It is very safe now. Don't worry," Claire said, glaring at Henri.

"Yes, yes, there is nothing to worry about, but you should have seen the mess. Claire and I were in our house with the windows closed."

Claire couldn't help herself and jumped in, "Because of the rain and cold. Then we heard something that sounded like a train traveling right next to us."

"It was very loud." Henri nodded in agreement.

"We do not have earthquakes, but I imagine it would feel like this. Just like you have in California," she said.

"Your house moved?" I asked.

"Well, no, but it was just like an earthquake in every other way."

"So, we look outside, all around our house, and then we see across the fence that the rocks and dirt had poured out into the grass, as if dynamite had exploded under this terrace," Henri continued.

"Why did it fall?"

"It happens. These stonewalls are very old. In Domme, there is a village committee that works on the village walls year round. The earth moves, and there is tremendous pressure on the rocks."

"So the village repairs the rock walls?"

Henri shrugged his shoulders. "It depends where the damage happens. If it is in a public area, then yes, the village repairs it."

Claire added, "Never quickly."

"If it happens between two properties on the same level, then the neighbors share the expense. If the properties are one above the other, then the rock wall is the higher property's responsibility to maintain and fix." Henri used his hands to diagram the situations.

"I think the rock work is beautiful, and I would love to have a stone house in California."

"Yes, but how long would you have it before an earthquake happens? Better to buy one in France," Claire said.

And we toasted to the dream of buying a house in France.

* * * * * * *

80

The time I had spent in New Zealand as a student cultivated in me a love of the sport of rugby. So I was very pleased to find a well-groomed rugby field and viewing stands on the outskirts of Cénac et St. Julien. It was within easy walking distance of my house. Even better was the timing of my arrival in Cénac—right during the first half of a promising season. The local lads were training hard, winning matches, and likely to be on their way to the championship. Almost every Sunday afternoon there would be a match, either in Cénac or in another village within the region which wasn't surprising, since rugby is considered the national sport, especially in the south of France. There are 1,737 rugby clubs in France, and the number of licensed players increases each year, reaching 390,000 in 2010.

The British introduced the sport to the French in the early 1870s. The first time it was played at the Olympics was in 1900 at the Paris Summer Games. The French won the gold medal. Since then, rugby has gained a popularity of its own and generated worldwide events. For example, in 2011 the Rugby World Cup came down to the final between France and New Zealand. Over 15.4 million people watched the match on French television and a considerable number traveled to New Zealand to witness the battle. The All Blacks of New Zealand were victorious. I was one of the few in California who woke at 2 a.m. and drove over the hill 15 miles from my warm comfy bed, to find a sports bar that had the cable network so I could watch the match live. I was emotionally invested in both teams because I had lived in both countries. Needless to say, it was a great match.

Rugby not only provided entertainment, but it also offered a chance to meet different members of the community, a reason to visit new villages during the away games, and of course an opportunity to have a conversation with new vocabulary. Family members of the players and rugby fans were scattered among the stands, although people tended to sit in the same place each week. In the upper west corner, I would always see the same group of teenage boys, hanging out, watching both the game and the young women. Down in the front two rows of the left section, a large family consisting of eight children and their grandparents attended to cheer on their dad. There were also two gentle, extremely patient caregivers, who led six disabled adults to the lower middle section every home match, making sure their wards were protected from the weather and enjoying the outing. I knew which spectators belonged to which players by their yells of encouragement or, in some cases, disgust. It was always a mixed crowd of men and women, old and young, those from the farm and those from town.

One Sunday, the tension in the air was particularly noticeable before the match. There was a larger than normal gap in the stands between the local fans and those from the visiting team. Evil looks were shot across to each other with the occasional insult. If I were witnessing an old, raw rivalry in the stands, what would happen on the field? The stout elderly woman with tight, dyed black curls and bright red lipstick with matching fingernail polish sitting next to me explained it to me.

"This team always is difficult. They are ..."

Her lips pushed together like she had eaten something sour. I didn't understand her word, but I knew it wasn't a compliment.

"They play in a bad way?" I asked. I made a mental note to look up the verb "to cheat."

"They play like animals, like they have no training, like they are not French."

"Oh."

People around us were listening to her as she picked up steam.

"You watch, they will do something dirty. I do not trust them. One year a player bit my son."

"I remember that," the man sitting behind us said.

"Wasn't that about five years ago?" his friend asked.

"He still has the scar!"

I didn't find out where the scar was located, thank goodness, because the whistle blew and the kick-off took place. The first half of the game had Cénac et St. Julien executing lots of hard tackles and skillful running to build the score to a substantial lead. By the middle of the second half, the other team was so frustrated that tempers were bound to flair. So it wasn't a big surprise when a late tackle knocked a player flat on his back, and a second sport emerged to take the place of the rugby: boxing. First all the players in the game jumped into the fight to defend their teammate. Then all the players along the sidelines, along with a coach or two, joined the fight. Now the field was one giant moving mob of arms and legs. Suddenly young men from the stands were leaping over the railing to get down to the field, young women were standing on the seats, screaming at their men on the team, and grandmas were bundling up little ones in their arms to take them away from the scene of violence. "I knew it! Didn't I tell you?" my neighbor in the stands turned away from me to direct her attention to the field, "Get away from him, you pig." Off she went down to the edge of the stands to make her comments heard.

I wasn't sure if the match was over or if I should stay in case play resumed.

"Is this normal?" I asked an elderly man who was calmly sitting off to the side.

"Fortunately, no," he said, "But people take their rugby seriously. It is a matter of pride between these two villages. Looking at them now you would not believe that many of these players work together or have known each other for generations. Maybe they are even related. On the rugby field, all else in life is forgotten."

After a short while, the referees were able to make people return to their proper places and the game continued. My former neighbor on the bench returned to her seat beside me, but the curls in her hair were not as tight as before.

"What did I tell you about those other players?" she huffed as she sat down, pulling her blouse in place over her stomach, "You see how it is."

And I had seen more than I wanted in this match of rugby and boxing.

* * * * * * *

Top Five Signs Becoming More French

#5. You are thinking and writing in English, but there on the page are a few French words, unconsciously written.

#4. You look at an English word and think, "That word needs an accent."

#3. You're more excited about your bread baker coming back from his vacation than you are about your upcoming weekend vacation. (The shop has been closed for TWO weeks.)

#2. You can calmly and nonchalantly walk through the shared area of the public toilets, past the men using the urinals, on your way to the women's stalls.

#1. You would rather eat cheese than chocolate.

* * * * * * *

Le Jour de la Libération on May 8th is a national holiday that celebrates the end of World War II. It is similar to Armistice Day; however, in France there usually is a presentation of Charles de Gaulle's famous 1940 speech recorded while he was in England as head of the Free French Forces, urging the French people to remain strong against Nazi Germany. Some historians credit his speech with igniting the resistance movement in France. In Domme, to celebrate the

holiday, the mayor, local veterans, all three members of the police department, the public, and the remaining local resistance fighters who proudly carried the national flags, were invited to the war monument for the ceremony. Every village in France had some kind of war monument, which listed the residents who died during the wars. The mayor spoke briefly, thanking those who fought for France and asked for a moment of silence for those who died in battle. Afterwards a recording of the national anthem was played. It was a somber, beautiful moment until the young boy by the car's loudspeaker took his hands away from covering his ears.

"*Maman*, that was too loud," he said.

When I told Emma that I attended the service with its unexpected spark of humor, she fondly remembered another service previous years ago.

"Even with all my years of living in France, I had never been to the service so I decided to go. I was the only member of the public, too, which I thought was pretty poor. Anyway, I was walking down the hill with the procession in the world's shortest parade—although there was a car in it this year only because John hurt his leg and couldn't walk—and I remembered that the short poles used to block the summer tourist traffic were up. To understand my *faux pas,* you have to know that those short traffic blocks are commonly referred to as '*bitte,*' or penis. Well, without thinking about it, I yelled to my friend who was walking beside the mayor, something like 'Stop! Look out for the *bittes.*' All the men checked their flies. Honestly, it was not my finest moment, but I was just trying to help."

On the back of a veteran's jacket is written "To never forget who we are," and having a ceremony to remember those who fought for their country is one way to do that. Another way in recent years is the national government's campaign to mark the sites where resistance fighters died. For too long, their ultimate contribution was not sufficiently recognized. The resistance movement is believed to have begun in the Dordogne Valley, and Emma's mother owned the remote farm where the first meeting of the resistance fighters took place.

"It is so fucking remote that the locals can't find it half the time. She's lucky she gets her mail. There was no way the Nazis would have found it."

Scattered around the region were plaques honoring those who bravely fought. A white headstone with a black plaque on a random corner told of a 80-year-old woman who was shot for smuggling food to the young fighters hiding in the hills, and another plaque nearby marked the spot where a 16-year-old boy was shot in front of his mother for not answering a German soldier's questions. I regularly walked past another plaque on the hospital's wall in Domme, each time I was on my way to class, and I asked Emma about it.

"That is an amazing story. About five or six summers ago, a tourist from Spain was walking by the hospital, and she just happened to read the plaque. She started to scream and her family didn't know what was wrong with her. It turns out that this was how she learned when, how, and where her brother was killed during the war. Just by reading the plaque. For so many years they had to live with not knowing what had happened to him. He was a freedom fighter from Spain, who came up to France to help in the resistance movement. Somehow, he got hurt and was in the Domme hospital. The Nazis heard about him, went in, and dragged him out of his hospital bed. They put him up against the hospital wall and shot him.

Of course his sister went into the mayor's office to get more information, and the following year the village invited her back for an official ceremony to honor her brother. It was so moving. Everyone was crying."

An unusual way to remember the past is to re-enact it, and that's what military enthusiasts did in their annual re-enactment of the battle to take back the bridge near Castelnaud from German control. The original battle was in 1944. As I walked through the staging area, authentic military equipment, uniforms, and flags represented France (military and resistance), the U.S.A., England, Germany, and Canada. All of the participants of the mock battle were native French, but from different areas of the country. They did not belong to re-enactment clubs but just shared a common interest in history and collecting military artifacts. One "American captain" told me that this year's attendance was lower than usual, because many had gone to the anniversary of the Normandy invasion earlier in the year. He also shared that playing the role of the Americans was the most popular; however, most people didn't mind being the Germans.

"Where did you find the jeeps and tanks in such perfect condition?" I asked.

"Oh, they weren't in that shape when we found them. Mostly we just found them in the countryside. Often it's necessary to order parts, but that's no problem."

"No offense, but do you think it is difficult for the people who lived through the war to see all of this?"

I was thinking of my elderly neighbor who lived up the hill from me. She refused to rent her holiday flat to any person from Germany, because during the war the Germans assassinated her brother. He used to row British soldiers and Jewish refugees over the channel to England, and one night upon his return to France, the German soldiers were waiting for him.

"Yes and no. There are people who will never come to this type of show because of difficult memories. I respect that. On the other hand, it is important to remember what happened. The lessons of history should never be forgotten."

* * * * * * *

"You watched at the bakery?" asked the chef of the La Traverse restaurant, sitting at one of his tables, stirring his espresso. He was wearing his usual startling white apron and creased black pants. Chef was meticulous about his appearance and his kitchen. His hairline may have been receding, but he always had a sharp haircut. He stared intently at me in a friendly way. I could practically see the wheels turning in his head.

"You should see a real French kitchen. Tomorrow, would you like to come to my kitchen during the midday meal? I will teach you how to make *Tourain Blanc*."

This was an invitation too wonderful to miss. La Traverse was my favorite restaurant and it just happened to be down the hill from our house. It was a local, year-round gathering place, and the owners were big supporters of the local rugby team, guaranteeing a crowd of players and fans on non-game days. There were wooden tables and chairs inside and out, a blue enamel stove for heat in the winter, and a string of small blue lights lit all year, draped in the corner of the bread station. The chalkboard always had the *plat du jour* listed. Ninety percent of the customers ordered the plate, because it was a great deal, homemade soup, small plate, main plate, cheese plate or dessert, and wine all for 13 euros. Coffee or an upgrade of the wine cost extra.

On the big day, I wore comfy shoes since I would be standing all day, and I tied my hair back. The kitchen was extremely narrow; stove on one side and cutting space and prep station on the other. Everything a chef might need was within easy reach. I arrived at 11 a.m. to find about 30 small plates prepped, dessert made, and cheeses sitting on the counter to become room temperature.

"Are you ready to learn how to make *Tourain Blanc*?" asked Chef. This warm garlic soup was a regional specialty. It had a mild yet full garlic flavor.

"Yes, I love the soup. I will write down all the steps," I said.

"Oh no, you will be the one making it for the lunch crowd, and they are all locals who know the soup. It is mother's milk to them."

Great. No pressure at all. He talked me through all the steps, and I manhandled the huge soup pot when necessary. I even performed the secret technique of stirring with force when adding the water to the garlic and flour mixture.

"The regulars will be happy with that soup and believe me, they are not shy when there is something they don't like," he said.

Monica, the petite whirlwind force of a waitress and all-around controller of the dining room snorted at his comment as she was putting the finishing touches to additional plates of the first course. She added an astute observation.

"When it is quiet for those precious few moments after the plates are delivered to the table, you know the guys are happy."

"Silence is golden?" I said.

"Silence is what I long for. But in this mad-house I will never get it." Her tone was one of affection and loving resignation. Monica was the heart of the restaurant. People came to La Traverse not just for the great food and prices, but also for Monica's spunk and sense of humor. She teased the regulars mercilessly as she took care of the 40 tables, and they teased her too, judging from the laughter that filled the room.

Monica was the daughter-in-law of the restaurant owner. If the restaurant was open, she was working. I had originally met her in the first month of my arrival, one Friday morning while reading the local newspaper in the bar of her restaurant. Even though it was 10 a.m., one young man who was a regular customer enjoyed a beer standing at the bar. He heard Monica promise to only speak French with me. When Monica stepped away to make my espresso, he leaned over to me and surprised me with a stage whisper.

"She is a good one, but do not trust her."

"You shut up." Monica obviously could hear us talking, even over the hiss of the espresso machine. I could tell from their relaxed, comfortable manner with each other that some friendly ribbing was about to include me.

"Why? What will she do?" I asked.

"I left my cell phone on the bar for just a minute. No, maybe for a few seconds and she played a joke on me."

Monica carried my coffee to me, laughing at the fond memory.

"He is a fool to leave his phone. I am an expert at texting. I am super fast. So I found what I thought was his ex-girlfriend's phone number and sent her a message. I said something like 'I still dream of you.' Well, it turned out to be her mother's number."

"I had a lot of explaining to do—to both of them—and I had never wanted to talk to her again. Just wait, Monica. I will get you back."

But when the noon meal approached, there was no joking around. Every day, the menu changed to reflect what was in season. For our day in the kitchen, the soup was *Tourain Blanc*, followed by the small plate of ham with corn and orzo salad, the main plate of roasted lamb with choice of couscous or *frites* (French fries), and finishing with dessert, which was a *crème brulee* tart.

On a typical day, the restaurant fed at least 80 people. This was a real French restaurant feeding French people who cared about their food and wanted to build a relationship with the chef. It was not a restaurant aimed at the tourist trade. The tradesmen and workers in the area came to Cénac et St. Julien to eat here, and only French was spoken. A friend told me that if I saw local license plates on the vehicles or many white vans of the tradesmen in the restaurant's parking lot, then I would know it was a good place to eat.

Chef handled the back of the house, and the two servers took care of the front. The noon meal was the main meal for many of the French, and they had at least two hours off from work to enjoy it. From noon to 3:00 p.m., the kitchen ran at a fast pace. Of the 80 or so meals served, only four were not from the *plat du jour* menu. During a brief, slow moment, I asked Chef if this small, but significant change in menus bothered him.

"I am here for the pleasure of the people. They are the kings. I only want to make them happy, and it's not about my ego. I would rather receive comments from my customers like 'Great meal' or 'You really made a super sauce' than receive money. But I have to feed my children, so I'll take the money," he said.

He nodded and smiled when I asked him if people requested favorite dishes when they saw him around town.

"It happens all the time, but I am always thinking about food, so it's okay."

Chef was calm throughout the meal service, even when his order wall was blanketed with order slips.

"It's easy, if you are organized," he said. There was singing and good spirits among the staff as food kept going out the kitchen door to the people.

"Now you can open a French café in California, and I will come to work for you," Monica said to me before she left the kitchen to deliver the last meal of the day.

"This place is in your blood," Chef yelled at her back. He turned to me, "She would never leave. It's in all of our blood."

I learned a few new vocabulary words and jokes while in the kitchen, but mainly I learned how wonderful it felt to be part of this community.

Tourain Blanc Du Périgord à La Traverse

ail (garlic)

farine (flour)

sel et poivre (salt and pepper)

eau (water)

oeufs (eggs)

D'abord couper l'ail et mettre en marmite dans de l' huile. Cuire jusqu' a ce qu'ils soient transparent. Ajouter beaucoup l'eau dans le marmite. A cote, melanger un peu de farine avec l'eau froide et quand bien mixer, mettre dans la marmite en brassant vigoureusement. Cuire a petit feu, jusqu' a epaississement.

Avant servir, ajouter un jaune d'oeuf soit casse par la chute, en brassant vigoureusement. Tres importante!

Tourne. Migoter a petit feu pour une heure.

First cut the garlic into small pieces. Put in pot with some oil. Cook until they change color to become transparent. Add a lot of water to the pot. At the same time, add the flour. Strong, forceful stirring is very important. Put on the stove at low heat.

Break the yolk into the pot from a high distance. It's very important that the drop break the egg yolk. Continue stirring. Simmer for an hour, and then serve.

* * * * * * * *

Sure, the goal was to learn another language, but beautiful France was just outside my front door. I had to explore! When I first arrived, I was very careful to keep two consecutive days each week free of any commitments, just so I could visit the numerous Châteaux, gardens, caves, and historical villages. France, especially the Dordogne, is so rich in interesting sites that it could take a lifetime to see it all, and I only had a little less than a year.

On my exploration days, the radio played the role of the teacher. Unfortunately, all my questions were ignored. I did enjoy the local area radio station though. The music selection was unconventional, the local news was very informative, and the editorials gave insight into the local attitudes. It seemed like politics, movies, and cooking were the most frequent subjects. The classroom was my destination, and my classmates were all the French people I met along the way, so chatting was encouraged. My textbook was the green *Michelin Guide*. Thirty years ago I bought all of the green *Michelin Guides*, each one explaining a different region of France, as a birthday gift for myself. Now I finally was going to use them instead of dust them. And use them I did.

"Karen, you are inspiring me to explore my adopted country. You've seen more of this region than I have, and I've lived here over thirty years," Hazel said in English at the start of a French class, "You are a good example for us Brits."

Emma was standing over by the file cabinet in our attic classroom, searching for a folder in the floor-to-ceiling stacks of books. She paused in her pursuit.

"Don't beat yourself up, Hazel. It's different if you know you have a limited time. Although, having said that, you are doing a hell of a good job, Karen."

"Thank you, both of you," I said. "I have to make every day count. The time will go by so quickly."

And the time did pass quickly, yet I made good use of it by exploring at least two to three new places every week. I enjoyed all of them. I dreaded it when people asked me what was my favorite place. I wanted to avoid making a choice.

"It would be easier to explain the meaning of life than to make me select my favorite place. I love them all!" I wanted to say, but normally I found myself answering with a different village each time. In my mind I knew that each location was receiving its due of admiration.

If I had to select three favorite places other than my village, my choices would be based on the beauty of the area and on my personal interactions with the residents.

The first place would be Saint-Avit-Sénieur during its annual antique fair weekend. This village is primarily known as a pilgrimage site for the walkers of Saint-Jacques de Campostelle, because of the 12th century church where a miracle took place. The antique market season in the

Dordogne ran throughout the spring and Saint-Avit-Sénieur kicked off the season with the late February, village-wide market. The vendors set up their tables and parked their merchandise-packed white vans along both sides of all the lanes. All the tops of the low rock walls were used to display merchandise; vintage clothing draped over some and oil lanterns balanced on others. Experienced vendors packed their area tightly, but with easily accessible walkways to sell as much as possible. It was one of the most anticipated antique markets of the year because of its size and rich variety of items.

The tables were filled with items such as antique glassware, tools, gold-framed mirrors, household knick-knacks, toys, and antique military weapons and medals. Large pieces of furniture, potbelly stoves, and bed frames were there too. Copper pots of every size and the large comical, green colored glass wine bottles used to age the wine in the sunshine, a process called "taking the wine for a walk," were favorites of mine. I walked up and down the streets examining each table. One time, I came close to buying an old-fashioned, round, box-shaped French police hat, but I hesitated. As I was talking with the seller, a short Frenchman wearing a fanny pack and a wildly colorful sweater, stopped me.

"Where are you from?" he wanted to know.

"California."

"I adore California. Honestly, I am California's number one fan," he said.

We spent at least thirty minutes talking about our favorite places in the world, food, our children, where to find the best Chinese restaurant, and politics until I asked him when he had visited California.

"Oh no, I only travel through my television," he said. "It is the perfect way of traveling without the risk, and I sleep in my own bed."

After saying good-bye, I continued shopping. On the outskirts of town, I noticed a van filled with merchandise, predominately metal outdoor furniture and garden ornaments. What caught my attention were the four vendors sharing a bottle of wine with snacks, laughing and enjoying the day, while waiting for customers. I wanted to capture their enjoyment of life in a photo, which brought me to their attention.

"Why not join us for a glass of wine?"

In California, I would have said "No, thank you," because of shyness and caution, but in France, joining them seemed like the perfect thing to do.

"We do four to five markets each year, and we have a store. Plus, we have to go to estate sales to buy," said Magali. "It is a busy but good life." Her huge smile and kind nature convinced me that she found joy and humor in day-to-day life.

"Do you sell a lot to international visitors or to the French?" I asked.

"We sell to both, but we love to hear the British and Parisian accents."

"Oh, especially the Parisians!"

"The price goes up!"

There was a roar of laughter and we toasted to Paris.

"Oh, Karen, look! You are seeing a truly French sight, one that is being lost. This is so traditional." Ever so slowly, walking up the lane, was a very short, hunched-over, grey-haired woman, dressed in her everyday farm work clothes and heavy-soled,

sensible shoes with a basket of bright yellow daffodils hanging from her arm. She was selling bunches of flowers from her garden. Magali approached the woman and kindly bought bunches for all of us. The transaction took awhile and then she walked back to us.

"I had a hard time understanding her," Magali said, "She mumbled in Occitan and French. Of course it would have helped if she had most of her teeth in."

My second favorite location was Collonges-La-Rouge, in the region of Limousin. It is a small village founded in the 8th century, entirely built out of red sandstone bricks. The communal bread oven still stands in the village square, sheltered by the timbered and slate tile roof. The 12th century church and manor Château added to the charm of the village that was known as a vacation destination for the wealthy.

I entered the mustard shop, more out of curiosity than need for mustard. There were so many bottles that lined the walls, could there be so many flavors of mustard? The young, red-haired shopkeeper was helpful and friendly. I asked about her unusual French accent, and she told me that her father was French and her mother was Scottish. They divorced when she was young, so she grew up in both countries and became bilingual by the age of eight. Our conversation remained in French though.

"You have good luck to learn French as a child. It takes me a long time to be at this point in French," I said.

"But you are doing the right thing in speaking French whenever you can. Do not be afraid to make mistakes."

We traded stories about the struggles of acquiring a different language, and she gave me strong words of encouragement. We shared many common experiences, and it was so fun to talk to someone who could relate to what I was going through that I didn't notice another customer waiting to pay. After making my purchase, I headed down the street only to be called back by the other customer in the mustard shop. I worried that he was angry.

"Excuse me. I heard what you said in the shop."

At this point, I was mentally trying to form an appropriate apology in French, one that this older French gentleman would accept. Before I could say anything, however, he completely surprised me.

"I never thought about how difficult it would be to learn French, or any language for that matter, and I admire your persistence. Good luck to you."

He shook my hand. I watched him walk away, and I was speechless in both languages.

The third and final location was Carcassonne, a well-preserved, medieval, fortified village in the Aude region, which attracted visitors from around the world. Walking along the outer walls that encircle the village, with their more than fifty towers, and through the inner-walled royal residence was like stepping back in time. In 1976, I had visited Carcassonne, so I was excited to see it again. Like any historical site that receives over three million visitors each year, there were bound to be too many tourist shops and restaurant barkers on the main cobblestoned streets. Taking the small lanes through the back neighborhoods helped ease the crowd pressures, and most people just ignored the magpie-like call of the restaurant barkers.

To me, however, sidewalk religious preachers, dinnertime telemarketers, and yes, even restaurant barkers were unlikely but extremely willing "French teachers" with their own agenda. I could look past all of those curricula in order to have a conversation. I had just rounded a corner on a tree-lined, but extremely narrow lane to see a small group of teenage restaurant workers sitting in mismatched chairs and one couch outside of their restaurant, smoking and chatting, when a pretty, long-haired woman in a medieval maiden costume noticed me and quickly stood up. She grabbed a menu with the same hand as her cigarette, smoke curling around the paper, and she faced me. Instead of my typical reaction in the U.S. which is to walk around them to avoid any interaction with the group, I stopped in front of them.

"We are open and *cassoulet* is the specialty of our restaurant. It is the best in Carcassonne," the woman said, with enough sincerity to make me think she was either related to or in love with the cook.

"I am not hungry. Yes, I am from California, but even I know it is too early to eat," I said with smile and a joking tone. They laughed since the punch line was the time of the day: 5:30 p.m. As I had hoped, the magic word worked again, and I was invited to sit with them, which I promptly accepted.

"Do all of you live in Carcassonne? What is it like to have these very old buildings be your home?"

There was a chorus of answers from "Have you seen the rest of France? We are a nation of old buildings, so we are used to them" to "I would love a modern bathroom" to "Americans throw too much away."

"Your French is not too bad," one sultry young man said with his cigarette still in his mouth, wearing ripped jeans and stretched full-length out on the couch.

"Don't be a shit," another said. "Her French is 100 times better than the usual tourist we get here and she is actually speaking French."

"No, it's okay. I know I still have a lot to learn. My French teacher in California spoke in English all the time. It was stupid, and I will never get that time in my life back again."

The "couch guy" sat straight up.

"Fuck. I had the same experience."

"Yeah, we thought your French was shit," one of his friends said. All of us laughed.

"My English teacher wasted my time. I learned more from television and music than from him."

The conversation continued until it was time for me to move on, but it was a pleasant way to spend an evening in a village where I'd heard more English, Japanese, German, and Dutch than I had for the last six months.

* * * * * * *

"Do you want me to get that spider, Emma?" I asked in English, before sitting down at the table at the start of class.

"No, no. She is part of my cleaning staff. Her web is catching all the bugs. It's my ingenious plan to avoid housework and let Mother Nature do it for me. Now class today is on something spicy."

But before the spice could be sprinkled upon us, Sue burst into class, breathless and upset. Normally Sue is cheery, always with an upbeat story about her gardening or her husband. It was the first time I had seen her so distressed.

"I am spitting mad at my grandson's teacher. You won't believe what she called him. I have a good mind to report her."

"Sue, whatever is the matter?" Hazel asked.

"That teacher is just too mean. It's not right what she did, and I don't care about respecting how a different country does things. Well, see for yourself." Sue thrust a paper in our general direction and kept talking. "My grandson is a good boy and he doesn't deserve this name calling. She called him a retard. Can you believe it? That's not okay in any situation, for any child."

"No, no one should be the target of name calling, especially not children by their teacher."

"That does seem harsh."

"That teacher should be fired!"

All of us were agreeing with Sue for moral support.

"Wait a minute," Emma said, "Let me read the letter from the teacher."

We were completely silent as Emma read the letter. Her Paul Newman-blue eyes darted back and forth across the page as she read. Finally, she put the page down, cleared her throat, and said in her most patient voice,

"Sue, this is just a misunderstanding. All your grandson's teacher is trying to tell you is that he is late to class, not mentally slow. There was no name calling."

"What do you mean?"

Emma handed her a French dictionary, the one that weighed at least 20 pounds. "See for yourself," she said.

"Oh, *retard* means late? Well, I guess I take back all my comments about her. Oh, I'm so glad I didn't go into the headmaster's office to file a complaint like I wanted to."

* * * * * * *

"Karen, do you believe in ghosts?" Colette asked me one afternoon, as Jean-Paul, Colette, and I were sitting at their kitchen table. They had been the perfect hosts to me so many times that I had brought them a loaf of homemade pumpkin bread to reciprocate their kind hospitality. It was still warm when I placed it in Jean-Paul's hands. He declared that we should eat some immediately. Plus, I think they were intrigued with the idea of bread made from a vegetable. Colette was a calm, intelligent person so I didn't take her question lightly.

"That is an interesting question. I do not know."

Jean-Paul raised his eyebrows as he chewed. He had a thought-provoking look on his face. I wasn't sure if it was due to his first taste of my bread or to his next comment.

"Americans believe in UFOs. They surely must believe in ghosts?"

I had to smile to myself. Countless times I was asked to explain something that, in the speaker's mind, related to all Americans. It would be impossible to squeeze all the differences found in America into one-concept-fits-all; people didn't realize the enormity of what they were asking me when they asked these nationwide-scope questions. At times like this, I felt I played the role of ambassador for America—as travelers always do whether they are aware of it or not—and I tried to be diplomatic.

"All Americans do not believe in UFOs, but yes, some people do. Many of the believers live in the southwest states, in the desert."

"Is this true? We, in France have a region where people believe in crazy things and do stupid things. It is called Paris; especially in the government buildings. By the way, this bread is very good—but next time you should add more vanilla," Jean-Paul said.

"Oh, thank you. Why do you ask about ghosts, Colette?"

I had been in France long enough to understand that I should not be offended by his evaluation of my baking. I knew his input was given out of kindness. Most French people care deeply about food. Jean-Paul was being a friend by giving me honest advice to improve my bread. Most of the time, the French are very direct and honest. (I realize the irony of making two sweeping statements about French people just now.)

"Yes, vanilla is the key ingredient. There should be more. Who would believe that pumpkin would make such delicious bread," Colette said. "Well, I asked about ghosts because Jean-Paul has shown you some interesting places, and now I have thought of an interesting place that I can share with you."

"Does it have a ghost?"

Jean-Paul reached for a second piece of pumpkin bread and said, "Yes, history says it does. I do not believe in such things. They are for children and bedtime stories."

"Yet when you drive us to the Château, you will wait in the car, no? If you do not believe in ghosts, why not walk through the castle with us?" Colette challenged him.

"I have serious reading to do." Jean-Paul smiled as he said this and winked at me.

"Ugh," Colette rolled her eyes at her husband. "Karen, I know one of the guides who works at a haunted Château not far from here, and she will take us on a private tour if you like."

"That would be super. Thank you, I would love to go."

We discussed the details, telephoned Colette's friend, and it turned out that the next day

suited everyone's schedule. A date to meet a ghost was arranged. Thank goodness they didn't line up our visit on a dark, stormy night. I've seen that movie, and it never ended well for the visitors.

Château de Puymartin is privately owned and the current owners, who are descendents of the original owners, live in one wing of the castle. In order to help with the high cost of owning a Château, the family opened up the haunted portion of the property to the public, allowing them to take guided tours. "Are you sure you do not want to come with us?" I asked Jean-Paul, right before we met Colette's friend.

"I have the newspaper to read with numerous stories about the economy. That is scary enough for me. Enjoy yourselves. I am happy to wait here."

Colette's friend soon arrived and after introductions were made, we started on our tour. The castle's spooky allure was immediately apparent as we entered the Château—the lighting fixtures were pale, white, feminine arms reaching out of the walls holding lit torches. We walked slowly, not only to allow Colette more time for her bad leg, but also so I could view the beautiful furnishings, tapestries, and architecture. The Château was built in the 13th century, and during the Hundred Year War it changed hands many times between the French and the English. That is why the intimate chapel near the main entry gate displayed old Catholic as well as old Protestant religious statues.

Madame led us through many warm, cozy rooms.

"The ghost lives in a very beautiful place," I said.

"Yes, but that was not always the case. Now we will enter the domain of her tragic past."

We started to climb the stairs of one of the towers. We climbed higher and higher, following the curve of the marble staircase, until we reached the top floor.

"It is a sad story, as often is the case with a wronged woman. The owner of the castle believed that his wife was unfaithful. There is no proof of that; yet he kept her in this bare, small room for fifteen years. She was completely alone during all that time. Look up at the trapdoor in the ceiling. This was how the food and water were lowered to her once a day. The servant was not allowed to talk to her. She had one small window from which to look out at life, and she stayed here until she died. If you touch this spot on the wall, you will feel an extreme cold. Nowhere else, on any of the other walls, at any time of day or night, can you find this extreme cold. Here is the essence of her spirit."

"Have you seen her?" I asked.

"Seen her, no. But many times while I was working in one of the rooms in this wing, I felt a strong presence in the room. One time, I was so sure a colleague was behind me that I started to talk to her. When I turned around, no one was there."

Colette and I looked at each other, smiling uneasily.

"Of course members of the family who own the Château have seen her. Adults and children describe her as the white lady who roams the hallways as if she is looking for something."

"I would like to see a ghost of a family member. Why are ghosts always someone you don't know?" I asked.

Colette crossed herself and told me to hush. "Do not wish for such things. Ghosts are serious."

"Colette, I did not know that you believe," her friend said. "What would your daughter, a respected scientist, say?"

"I believe many things that science has yet to prove or disprove." She shrugged her shoulders and continued, "It doesn't hurt to honor the traditions of All Saint's Day and *Le Jour Mort*."

"Yes, I use The Day of the Dead as a reminder to tidy my parents' grave, but do you follow the old practices of the holiday?"

I didn't recognize either holiday, so I was very interested in their exchange.

"I used to set a place at the table, but I never left the front door open. Then Jean-Paul told me to stop with all the silliness."

"Excuse me. I'm sorry, but I don't understand. Why do you do these things?" I asked.

"I do not anymore. It is an old belief that the night of *Le Jour Mort* is a special time when the distance between this living world and the spirit world is very thin: thin enough for the spirits to cross over. These gestures of an open door or a place at the table are signs to our deceased loved ones that they are welcome and not forgotten. Cemeteries are groomed and decorated with many small white candles to help the spirits find their way home." Again Colette shrugged her shoulders. "It is mainly a nice opportunity to stop and think of loved ones who have passed on."

Colette's friend reached out to reassure her by rubbing her upper arm.

"*Exactement.* Now let me show you one more thing that the owners are scared of, but it will not bother either of you, I promise."

We slowly climbed one more flight of stairs into the attic, where the underside of the slate stone roof shone through the thick wooden beams. The space was dry, even though it had started to rain. Very little light was visible through the seams where the stones overlapped.

"You see the original roof above you. It is a masterpiece of traditional stonework and if, or I should say when, the owners need to replace this roof, it will cost well over a million euros."

"Oh, I would be more afraid of that than the white lady too," I said.

Back at the Château's front door, we thanked our guide for the tour and before leaving I told her, "I think tonight I will have nightmares."

"If you see a ghost, I hope it is a dear family relative," she said.

"Yes, but that means he is in France, so I would speak French to an American ghost."

Jean-Paul was still reading in the car when we returned. He looked up when he saw us coming towards him.

"Now are we are finished with this ghost business? Let's go home."

* * * * * * *

I had become caught up in the World Cup, like the rest of Europe. One night I was watching the match between the U.S. and Portugal when a lightning storm knocked out my TV connection. My attention shifted to watching the storm rage for hours, but I wondered how the U.S. team was doing. So the next morning, when I was waiting in line at the butcher's shop, I tried to read about the match from the open sports page, which rested behind the meat counter. I stood on tiptoes and twisted my neck, but it was still too difficult to read. The butcher noticed me trying to see the newspaper. All meat business stopped.

"Do you like football?" he asked with a hint of disbelief. He knew I was American.

"Yes, I do. I was watching the U.S. play last night, but the television stopped working because of the storm," I said.

"Oh shit, that's awful." He reacted like I had told him a friend had died. "I will find the results for you," he offered. The duck for the man at the front of the line was put down and the search for the U.S. results began, much to the dismay of the hungry customer. The butcher carefully scanned each page of the thick newspaper while the line of customers grew. He was a kind man-on-a-mission. When I dared to turn around to check how long the line had grown, I saw that it had reached the doorway extending six people long.

"I'm sorry," I mouthed to the customers.

The people waiting were very nice about it and very patient. "Oh, this is very normal during World Cup," one woman said, shrugging her shoulders. The butcher hit the newspaper with his hand and at the same time said, "I think the U.S. team lost." Then it was my turn to say "shit," which got a laugh from the crowd. The butcher was willing to continue searching to find the exact score, but I reassured him that I could find the score online.

Every time I went into the butcher shop there was always time for a conversation, whether brief or long. He wanted to know where I was from, what Californians ate, why Americans didn't like football more, and why I wanted to learn French. We talked about many things. Who would have believed that the World Cup would help me learn French?

* * * * * * *

The closed hotel at the bottom of the hill along the main road had boards nailed across most of the windows. The building had faded paint and chipped, cracked plaster that announced its long period of inactivity. The hotel sign no longer shouted for attention. The small areas of garden with roses were cared for, but otherwise the business looked abandoned and forgotten. I walked by it many times, never looking at it twice. One day, as I passed by, I saw an elegantly dressed older woman standing on the front step, leaning on the railing. I was curious and concerned about her because she looked lonely, so I started a conversation. I discovered that she lived in the house attached at the back of the hotel and that she was the owner of the building. She asked questions about me too, and we had a nice visit. It was so pleasant that I returned several days later with homemade chocolate chip cookies as a "thank-you-for-listening-to-my-bad-French" gift. My intention was just to stay for a second, since I didn't have an invitation, but she graciously proposed that we sit on the balcony for another visit.

"You have a wonderful view of the river from here," I said to her, as we talked over sweet chestnut liqueur and cookies.

"Yes, the location and my mother's cooking were what brought people here to my family's hotel. I was born in this hotel."

"That's amazing. It's sad that the hotel is closed."

"It is sad, but no one in the family wants to run it. In its day, the hotel was very famous. Would you like to see the hotel's album?"

"Of course. Thank you."

She carried to the table an extremely thick, leather-covered album and placed it in front of me. I slowly turned page after page of thank-you notes written to compliment the high quality service and cuisine. Then I noticed a particular letterhead on one note: Buckingham Palace. In 1968, Prince Charles and his entourage had stayed at the hotel.

"Did you meet Prince Charles?"

She wasn't hesitant to answer; her memories were clear.

"My mother did, but no, I didn't. We had so many nice people stay here. I remember meeting Brigitte Bardot. She was a very sweet girl who appreciated everything. We had the actors from the movie *A Bridge Over The River Kwai* who were no trouble. You know, sometimes actors can be a problem. We had famous poets and musicians. One jazz musician liked to practice on the terrace."

I turned another page to see the Rockefeller family letterhead.

"It is like the history of the hotel is the history of the world," I exclaimed, a bit star struck.

She sighed and said, "It was another time, an exciting time. My mother was an excellent cook and won awards. She used local fish and vegetables. Only fresh, local items were used, and she made the products of this region famous. Parisian chefs came here to learn from her."

"That is very impressive."

Madame told me many stories, and she laughed often at the memories we stirred. I wish that I could have understood every word she said. I felt very honored to receive her hospitality. As we said our good-byes, she said to me, "When you stopped the first time, I liked the twinkle in your eyes and your spark of life. You keep that."

* * * * * * *

It was just after our class mid-lesson break, so the wine bottle was open, glasses were full, and sack lunches were spread on the table. Our notebooks and pens were off to the side, waiting for work to resume. Hazel was in the corner, searching for an English book to borrow from Emma's stack of novels. The tower of books made a mockery of the Leaning Tower of Pisa, so that Hazel was a bit nervous about touching a book. Emma had a hairpin in her mouth as she twisted her long blonde hair to the top of her head to pin it, but that didn't stop her from recommending a book for Hazel to read. Much to Hazel's dismay, it was towards the bottom of the stack. Emma told her not to worry about knocking the books over because that spilled book display would match the rest of the room. Sue was telling me about her grandson's music lessons, which reminded me of Emma's show.

"Emma, I know you have a music show soon, but I forget the day. When is it?" I asked in French.

"Karen, be careful how you say 'when'! I don't think I deserved that," she said in English with a smile, referring to my pronunciation of *'quand'*.

"Oh no. I didn't. I'm sorry."

"Remember, think of *Star Trek* and *The Wrath of Khan* when you say 'when' to get the correct sound, not 'con' or else you would be calling someone an asshole unintentionally."

"Thinking of actors reminds me of your trick how to remember the word for bullshit: Sean Connery," I said thinking of the word *'conneries'*.

"Well, anyone who would say a woman should be hit from time to time is full of bullshit," Emma said.

"Emma, what were those tricks you gave the class months ago, but I was absent that day?" Sue asked when she realized that she missed many of our memory tricks to remember French words.

"There have been a lot of tricks, Sue. Do you know what they were about?"

"Tricks to help remember if things are masculine or feminine. Oh, and there was one to help remember if you use *être* or *avoir* to help make a verb in the past tense."

We returned to our seats and quickly found our pens.

"When I'm at the grocery store, and I don't know if an item is masculine or feminine, I just order two of them. That avoids that pesky problem of *'une'* or *'un,'*" Hazel said.

"Or you could say *'du'* for some," I offered.

Emma shook her head.

"Yes, but how many pineapples or watermelons do you really need or want? There are times when you should be able to request just one. Here's what I have found: fruits, vegetables, the rivers in France, flowers, and clothes are feminine, if the word ends with an 'e.' It took forever to think of an exception, and I even had the grocer and his wife thinking about it too. One day she came up to me and said, *'le pamplemousse,'* and we laughed. Years later when she passed away, I placed a grapefruit among the flowers at her grave. That looked crazy, I'm sure."

"Or maybe they thought it was an old British custom," Sue said.

"Those fucking mad British at it again," Emma laughed. "They probably did think that or, more accurately, mad Emma is at it again. Anyway, another rule is that all calendar dates are masculine."

"I could use help with the question of using 'être' or 'avoir' too. Usually I just use 'avoir,' but I know that's lazy," I said.

"Well, about 90% of the time 'avoir' is correct, so you're not too far wrong. When I was in college, or high school for my American friend, I created 'Mr. Van's Tramped' as a tool to help me remember the verbs that use 'être.' There is a pattern to those verbs."

She turned to the white board, took her ripped, plaid shirt off the back of the chair to use as the eraser and then wrote the following chart.

M	monté	went up
R	rentré	went home
V	venu	came
A	allé	went
N	né	born (the ultimate went in)
S	sorti	went out
T	tombé	fell down
R	retourné	went back
A	arrivé	arrived
M	morti	died (the ultimate went out)
P	parti	went off on holiday
E	entré	went in
D	descendu	went down

"This is fantastic. Why didn't my high school teacher give us this stuff?" I whined. "Do you have other tricks, Emma?"

"There are no tricks other than keep at it, love. Every time you speak, you're helping yourself."

"*Nous sommes tellement…*," Sue started to say when Emma interrupted her.

"No, we are not '*nous*' here. It is more inclusive to say '*on*.' When a group of French friends speak of their group, they always use '*on*' like '*on doit retourner au travail*.'" (We must return to work)

Emma raised her eyebrows and looked at us.

"Are you ready to get back to the subjective tense? The French love it. You will hear it all the bloody time. *Maintenant on va commencer*." (Now we are going to start.)

Later that afternoon, I was walking down the narrow street in Domme, just after leaving Emma's house, when a car slowed down beside me. The window rolled down and the driver asked me a question that in summertime is the most important question on everyone's mind. He thought I looked like the person with the secret wisdom.

"Excuse me. Do you know where I can park?" And you know, he was right. I did know, but the price for gaining that information was participating in a French conversation with me. We talked, and I shared where he could find parking spaces for free and for a fee. I had hoped to use a word I just

learned in class, but he didn't do anything to deserve being called an asshole.

* * * * * * *

Top Seven Signs of Becoming A Local

#7. You know the names and shapes of 10 breads.

#6. You have visited all the locations in the French historical graphic novel about this region and you can read it too.

#5. You make your own salad dressing by mixing walnut oil, vinegar, walnut mustard, and a little sugar.

#4. You avoid going into or near Sarlat towards the end of July and all of August because of traffic. Yesterday we saw a 4-mile backup of cars.

#3. You no longer mind that your driveway is on a super narrow, steep lane on the side of a mountain, with a dangerous drop-off on one side. Sometimes the side mirrors are even left fully extended, just to add a bit more challenge.

#2. You have a favorite *foie gras,* which is only sold directly from the farm and requires a 30-minute drive into remote country to obtain.

#1. Best of all, you have conversations in French with others who aren't slowing down their speech, and they often compliment your French.

* * * * * * *

When I selected the Dordogne Valley as my new home for a year, I was aware that a world-class region of wine was close by. Anyone who has sniffed a glass of wine or marveled at the color of a full-bodied red recognizes the Bordeaux area as a region of superior wines. But it also is a region of superior prices. What I was looking for was an everyday wine. One that had good taste and an acceptable price; something more than the wine out of the "gasoline pump" at the wine store, but less than the ten-year-old, cellared bottle from a Bordeaux estate. Don't get me wrong; I drank the bulk *cave* wine often. Just now and again, I desired a more refined wine.

I discovered a new type of wine and the perfect winery, with the help of a wonderful fictional character, Bruno Courrèges. Martin Walker is the author of the *Bruno, Chief of Police* series based in a fictional village in the Dordogne Valley. The highly entertaining stories are murder mysteries, but the reason I liked them so much is that the writing was filled with realistic details and characteristics of life in France. Mr. Walker is the first of very few foreigners to have received the honor of being named the *Grand Consul de la Vinée de Bergerac*. It is obvious he instilled his knowledge of wine in his main character, since in every one of his seven books, Bruno drinks Pécharmant wine from Château de Tiregand. I took Mr. Walker's sound advice and searched for his favorite winery.

The Pécharmant wine region is found just to the northeast of Bergerac. In 1946, the national government granted AOC status (*Appellation d'Origine Controlée* which means Controlled Name of Origin) to the 441 hectares devoted to the careful cultivation of wine grapes, thereby insuring that only those wines produced in this region would be recognized as Pécharmant. Similar protection exists for champagne, Roquefort blue cheese, chickens raised in the Bresse region, and many other French products. Only 46 producers grow Pécharmant wines, and it takes six to seven years for a new vine to mature and reach its peak. The vintners believe the key element to making excellent wine is the composition of the soil. Having a sufficient amount of iron in the soil, sometimes due to the erosion of buried pre-historic artifacts, is essential. Pécharmant wines are created from a blend of Merlot, Cabernet Franc, Cabernet Sauvignon, and Malbec grapes, and it was a particular blending recipe of Château de Tiregand that earned my favor.

Château de Tiregand had won numerous awards, but the most important thing to me was the taste. It really was that simple. I appreciated that they picked the grapes by hand, only in the morning, and that their ancestor was Antoine de Saint-Exupéry, the author of the literary classic *The Little Prince*, but really the most relevant information about the wine was coming to me from my taste buds. It was truly delicious and very reasonably priced.

I was halfway through the free tasting when a large group of Americans entered the small stone tasting room. They didn't respond to Monsieur's or my *bonjour*, and I watched them look around the tasting room. Monsieur invited them to join our tasting, and they eagerly accepted. After sampling only three wines, they had become self-appointed experts and were quick to offer advice on how to make wines that would "compare to the ones back home." I cringed inside, but remained silent. Then one of the women noticed me. She thanked me for including them in my tasting and then apologized for not speaking French.

"That isn't a problem. I'm from California."

"Oh, you're American. I thought you were French."

Well, my opinion of her changed. Now she was insightful and kind, but did I really look French? I definitely felt comfortable in this culture, and I was wearing scarves more often mirroring the typical French person's love of scarves. We shared travel stories about France, and I learned that she had spent a year in Paris about twenty years earlier. After hearing this, I shifted our conversation into French, not wanting to waste any opportunity. I was shocked by her accent, and at first I thought she was playing a joke. It was like a South Park parody of a person trying to speak French. The other thing I noticed was to be expected after a long period away from the language: she had forgotten basic words. She illustrated a valuable warning to me of the importance of practicing my French once I've returned to California.

* * * * * * *

I had just walked down the steepest part of the back road from Domme to Cénac et St. Julien, coming home from my French class, when I saw Jean-Paul standing in the intersection. The stray, but extremely friendly, skinny neighborhood cat was rubbing against his legs. Months before Jean-Paul told me that one of our neighbors who used the Cénac et St. Julien home as a vacation house had abandon this cat. The cruel behavior upset Jean-Paul. Upon hearing this I started buying cat food for her and I suspected Jean-Paul fed her too. Before Jean-Paul noticed me, I watched him gently petting the cat, even though previously he had told me that he didn't like cats.

"Oh, here you are. I am waiting for you because my friends are doing something very interesting that you should see."

"Thank you. It is kind that you think of me."

Normally at this intersection, I would have turned right towards my home, but I followed Jean-Paul to the left, down to his place. The kitty trotted along with us.

"What are your friends doing?"

"They are working in the old way, and I thought of you. Do you have your camera?"

"My camera and my dictionary are always with me."

"Good. Then we are ready."

Before entering his home, I dug to the bottom of my book bag to retrieve another item I always carried: dry cat snacks. I quickly tossed out a few morsels to the sweet tempered stray that I had covertly named Josephine and turned towards his front door.

"No, we will drive to my friend's barn. It is not too far."

We drove just outside of the village, past the church, down a dirt lane through the walnut orchards, to arrive at a large wooden shed. The double doors were wide open to reveal a mill grinding stone, a large press, a deeply scarred wooden table, numerous buckets, and many clean bottles. Two of Jean-Paul's friends were already at work preparing the grinding stone.

"They are making walnut oil the traditional way. The mill and the press are very old, but they work perfectly."

After introductions were made, the workers took quick puffs on their cigarettes, and then it was back to work.

"The walnuts were already shelled and heated by the women earlier today. They made sure not to heat the walnuts too much or the taste will become bitter."

"How hot is necessary?"

"About 80 to 82 degrees C, so all the moisture is evaporated."

Now the mechanized, top upright millstone was slowly rolling around the bottom millstone, crushing the walnuts as it rotated. When it looked like all the walnuts were pulverized, the mixture was collected and put into a cotton cheesecloth. The wrapped package was placed in the press for the next step. This press had a motor to slowly lower the plate, squeezing the mixture until the golden oil started to pour out of the drain into the bucket. Older models of the press used harnessed horses to lower the plate. Once the oil stopped dripping, the cakes of pressed walnuts were returned to the grindstone. A little water was added, and the process was repeated one more time in order to obtain all the oil from the nuts. When the oil bucket was full, it was poured into the prepared clean bottles where the natural walnut oil settles and clears. Jean-Paul told me that about eight pounds of walnut meat produces two quarts of walnut oil. Walnut oil is one of the healthiest and tastiest of oils. It contains calcium, zinc, iron, magnesium, niacin, Vitamin E, B-1, B-2, and B-3.

This glimpse into the past reminded me of another enjoyable day, spent at the Fête à l'Ancienne in Cénac et St. Julien. It was a two-day festival that brought to life the traditional ways of old. The Cénac et St. Julien rugby team had organized the event as a fundraiser. Some of the locals dressed in the ancient costumes of their grandparents, which featured handcrafted, white lace caps for the women, lace petticoats peeking under the long dark skirts, dark blue blouses with lace collars large enough to cover their shoulders, and lace trim on the women's aprons. Old farm equipment, vintage cars, and ancient, large, front-wheeled bicycles were displayed around the grounds.

The main attractions were the stations where a craft or skill was being demonstrated. Two men, one with a cigarette dangling from his mouth, hand-carved a *fleur de lys* from a chunk of limestone, a detailed pencil sketch drawn on the same stone promised more artistry to come. Another station had a man manipulating very thin strips of wood into furniture, and opposite him two women operated the apple press, making natural apple juice. The highlight of the fair with the biggest crowd around it was the old copper still. The elderly couple who owned the still also sold their sweet, fortified, walnut wine out of the trunk of their car. I bought a bottle, and I was very happy to report that no hair grew on my chest after drinking it. I had enjoyed the demonstrations, sampled the wine, listened to the music, and was about ready to walk home,

when I saw Monica, her rugby-player husband, and her father-in-law across the grounds. This was perhaps the final opportunity to say thank you for their friendship and wonderful meals. Several months ago, their restaurant La Traverse inexplicably closed for good. A local favorite and thriving restaurant was no more, and no one knew why.

"I am so happy to see you. I have great memories of your restaurant."

I wanted to say that I missed it, but I worried that I might use the inappropriate slang meaning of the verb with sexual overtones. I didn't want to accidently repeat that mistake.

"It is too sad. We have nothing now, but it is just one of those things. I must accept it." Her eyes were watering, and she looked away. It wasn't the time to ask for an explanation of the fate of their restaurant.

"It was a wonderful place, and I feel lucky to have known it and you. I wish good luck for you very soon," I said. I didn't know what to say to soften the pain of loss, nor how to express how truly remarkable I thought she was.

"Thank you. It was like a second home to me. Now that it is gone..."

I gave her a hug.

"Things will be better."

"Things must be better. If not, I will come to California, eh?"

A couple of weeks later, I sat in the other café in my village, with my newspaper and dictionary, about to enjoy my favorite Friday routine. I tried to quiet my mind and adjust to the new environment. Sometimes change was difficult. I had frequented this café enough for the owner and his family to recognize me, but it still didn't feel as comfortable as the other café. When the owner brought my espresso over to me, on a whim, I asked him for his thoughts.

"What do you think happened over there at La Traverse? Why did they close?"

It was like I had asked this 70-year-old man, why do women find him so attractive and smart? He threw down the serving cloth and pulled out the chair opposite mine. He was ready for a quality gossip session. As he sat down, he rolled up his sleeves and started talking.

"It is a mystery, but I think I know."

"They were always busy and the food was super."

"Yes, but I think something was not right over there. Maybe they fed too many people without charging enough or ...."

He had more theories and, judging from his body language, leaning forward, elbows on the table, and eyes wide open, he was just warming up to his grandest theory. There was a day in my past when I would have been so happy to gossip in French, but now I felt sad, because I knew the loss behind the words.

* * * * * * *

Whenever I walked or drove by the closed hotel at the bottom of the hill, I always slowed down to look for my hotelier friend. Her small patch of roses looked well cared for, so I knew the opportunity would come for another casual visit. Sure enough, about a week later, I saw her deadheading her roses. Since I was not on my way to class or an appointment, I stopped to see her again.

"Bonjour. Are you well?"

"It is good to see you again. Have you learned a new French word today? Is your brain thinking in French now?" she asked.

"Oh, I wish that was true, but no."

"It will come. Have courage."

"I thought, maybe, you would like to see pictures of my daughters like I promised at our last visit."

"Do you have them now? That would be wonderful. Come, we will sit in the shade."

We spent an hour exchanging family pictures and giving compliments to each other's children. Accomplishments and personality traits of the children were explained. This shared time was a blessing to both of us; my mind benefited from the French conversation, and she, I hope, benefited from the companionship.

"I continue to think about your hotel. You must have other Americans besides the Rockefellers? (I wasn't sure how to say "must have had;" it was a little too complicated.) Do you remember anything special about those American visitors?"

"The only thing that comes to mind is how friendly the Americans were. Very nice people, as a rule."

"Well, that is good."

"Also as a rule, Americans had problems understanding what the bidet was for. Well, I was a young woman, and I didn't want to explain it to a grown man. So if anyone asked me about it, I would just agree with his guess. It was easier that way."

"Normally one doesn't find a bidet in an American bathroom."

"And I could tell when an American person or family were sitting by the pool, because they were the ones uncomfortable with the topless sunbathers."

"We do not treat nudity the same way as the French. It is true," I said.

"It is a body, and it is natural."

I thought, how French this is to have a conversation with a seventy-year-old woman who encourages nudity and being comfortable in one's body. I didn't have the heart to tell her my shopping-for-a-swimsuit story, but I think she would have laughed.

* * * * * * *

French politics briefly entered my life in June when I was invited into Jean-Paul and Colette's house for drinks, and the mayor of Cénac et St. Julien was a guest too. He lived across the lane from them in a two-story stone house with about thirty flowerpots around the front, filled with red geraniums. As I walked by his house regularly, I often wondered why a transplanted dead tree, with a faded, torn, tricolor banner hanging from it, had been left by his front door. This dead limb seemed out of place in a garden filled with color and life.

Dropping by for a quick drink was something that the mayor apparently often did, because Jean-Paul knew what his drink of choice was without asking. He was a soft-spoken, quiet man - not common traits of a politician, yet he was up for an easy re-election, so he must have been doing something right. Being mayor of Cénac et St. Julien was only part of his work; he also ran a catering business.

"I need to find three good women," he quietly said, as Jean-Paul handed him a generous pour of *pastis*. Since I had been given the same thing, I carefully watched the mayor pour water in his glass for the perfect ratio. I tried to copy him and was very happy with the results. The semi-sweet, strong black licorice taste surprised me as much as the mayor's comment. He didn't appear to be a player. He turned to me and asked with a shy smile, "Do you know where I can find them?" Was he asking me what I thought he was asking me?

"I don't understand," was my answer, but this time it was not because I didn't understand the French. I just didn't understand what he was getting at.

"No? It is election time, and each year we search for people to be on the city council."

Colette explained further, "On every city council there must be an equal number of female councilors and male councilors. It is always seven and seven. Other villages may select their mayor differently, but we use the system where the elected councilor with the highest number of votes becomes mayor. The only exception would be if the person is not a native of France."

Jean-Paul picked up from there, "Only the French can lead France! We are happy to let those who have moved to the wonderful French way of life help serve in the council, but they may not lead. The U.S. does the same, no?"

"Yes, that's true only for the president. How long is the service?" I asked.

"Some days it feels like forever." Again the mayor's shy smile appeared. "Most times it feels like what it is: an honor. And that honor lasts for two years."

The election was scheduled to take place in four weeks, and I asked the mayor if I might sit in City Hall to observe the voting. He was standing, about to leave to return to an event he was catering, but he stopped. "Of course. Democracy is something we in France never take for granted. You may observe, but do not interfere."

He muttered something else about Americans interfering as he left, but it's probably a good thing I didn't catch it.

Unlike a typical American town at election time my village looked the same before, during, and after the election. There were no candidate's signs in people's yards, no radio ads about the merits of one candidate or the weaknesses of another. The only nod to the election was when the local newspaper had interviews with the candidates. It also printed the complete list of names of all who were running in the two groups. The groupings had nothing to do with each person's political party affiliation; in villages of 1,000 people or less, people vote their council members in as a group, not as individuals. However, people do have the right to cross off a name in the group and may write in a name. If one list does not have a majority by the end of the voting day, then the election continues for a second round of voting within seven days.

"I remember," Emma told me the day before the election, "when the election was really strange. Well, it's usually fucked up, isn't it? But in this case it worked out. A guy in Domme who was particularly liked and smart won the election as a write-in."

I entered City Hall on election-day morning, not sure what to expect. The plain, window-filled room had four long tables formed in a "U" shape, with two large, glass boxes at the base of the "U." Two men were standing behind the glass boxes, while two women were handling the paperwork associated with voting at the end of the "U." The happy gathering of voters stood in line, most holding their completed, sealed ballots, visiting with one another while waiting for their turn with the glass box. No one was in a hurry. People working at the election visited with voters as well. I noticed that there were two colors of ballots, each with its own transparent box. Once the voter reached the glass boxes, he or she dropped the ballot into the appropriate one, and the official loudly announced "*A voté*" which meant, "Your ballot has been cast." It is an old tradition and purely ceremonial. Afterwards the voter moved on to the next station to register the vote. There were two small booths for privacy while voting called an *isoloir*, if a person had not completed their ballot. The process was formal yet friendly at the same time.

Months after all the votes were in, counted, and the results announced, a final political ceremony was performed. It was the *Plantation Des Mais Des Élus*. The Planting of the Corn of the Elected was a series of public ceremonies, where a young, rootless, evergreen tree was planted in front of each of the fourteen newly-elected's homes or businesses. The whole process took several weekends. The tree was a symbol of community service, and it stood to honor the elected's gift of time and work. After a short time, the rootless tree would die, but the French colors and the words on the plaque, "To Honor Our Councilor," would remain in the place of honor.

"Are you coming this Saturday?" Claire asked me. "You can ride with me."

"Oh yes, I really want to see the ceremony of *Plantation des Mais des Élus*," I said.

"You know this Saturday there will only be four ceremonies, so it will be a quick day."

Now I had been in France long enough to know that there would be nothing quick about a French ceremony, let alone four of them.

"Well, Claire, thank you very much for your kind offer, but I better drive myself. I can only go to one because my parents are visiting."

"Karen, do as you must, but you will miss some good fun and champagne."

Claire was right once again.

It was a poignant ceremony with delicious champagne. The event started with all the newly elected members, their families and friends, supporters, and community members who are interested, or maybe just thirsty, arriving at the new councilor's home. Even though most had just seen each other at another councilor's home not two hours before, greetings of kisses and handshakes were still given. I was graciously introduced to the newly elected councilor and Claire introduced me to several other people as well. As people visited and ate, others carried the long slender tree into the yard. It was time to prepare the tree. First, all of the limbs on the lower half of the tree were removed. Then other councilor members, along with the mayor, tied a circular banner in the French colors (red, white, and blue) around the tree trunk and nailed the plaque to the tree. The planting hole had already been dug, so all the newly elected joined together to raise the tree and plant it in the hole. It was a moment reminiscent of the famous photograph of the U.S. marines at Iwo Jima.

Once the tree was planted straight, and numerous other branches from neighboring trees were pruned away for better visibility, the council reached for the champagne bottles and gathered under the newly-planted tree. The crowd quieted and stepped closer, glasses in hand. Each councilor poured a glass of champagne for another councilor. There still was complete silence. The mayor stepped forward, slowly walked over to the proud symbol of community, and poured his glass of champagne onto the tree trunk. The councilor who lived at this house was second to pour her glass on the tree, and the others followed suit.

Claire whispered to me, "The first glass is given to the tree to symbolize a toast to the community. The new councilors are showing us that they will put the community first before anything else."

Back under the tree, the city council and the mayor poured a second round for each other. Again the mayor stepped forward with glass held high. He turned towards his council and to deliver his toast.

"We drink to each other. May we work in good faith and good spirit for the benefit of our community."

The councilors quietly echoed his wishes then drank, but the audience was completely silent.

"Now it's our time for a *'verre de l'amitié,'*" (a glass of friendship) whispered Claire, who again was close to my ear. There was no need to whisper though, because the crowd was familiar with the ceremony. Like magic, it roared into action. Glasses were filled, laughter was heard, and many admired the tree.

* * * * * * *

"If you want *terroir*, then you have got to go there and eat," Emma told me. She continued, "It is earthy and real, and it's like what France used to be before the fucking plastic franchise restaurant chains invaded."

"That sounds perfect," I said.

"It's in a *bled* though, so it's hard to find."

"Eh, what's a *bled*?"

"*Un bled* is a bum fuck, nowhere, little one-horse town."

"Oh, got it. I'll use the GPS."

"You're going to love it."

And Emma was right about all of it. My husband and I drove through the beautiful countryside of walnut orchards, corn, and fields of sunflowers meandering along the narrow lanes without a clear sense of direction. Then, as we rounded a wide curve where four stone buildings were grouped, there was the sign announcing Chez Nicole. It looked like a normal stone house that closed its shutters against the midday sun to keep the cool air inside. The few tables outside under the yellow awning were empty except for a lone lizard basking in the sun. Three small dogs had each found a different grassy place in the shade to nap. Our arrival interrupted their sleep. The gravel parking lot held several dirty, dented French vans. A van in a restaurant's parking lot is always a good sign.

I walked into the restaurant to find the 80-year-old owner/chef Nicole standing beside a table of six middle-aged men wearing overalls, telling them a hunting story. The men were enjoying the soup and the story.

"Hello," I said to everyone in the room, because it was only polite. "Do you have a table for two, please?" I asked.

"Do you have a reservation? Did you telephone?" Chef Nicole asked with a smile.

"No, I'm sorry. I did not."

"Well, I can feed you with the bottom of the pan," she said with a twinkle in her eye. She and the little ungroomed dogs that gave up on their naps, led us over to a table with fresh flowers in the middle. We didn't wait long before a big tureen of homemade garlic soup was brought to the table. Homemade bread quickly followed. The second plate was a cold veggie salad with a slab of homemade pork paté beside it. Little dill pickles circled the plate. The dogs were especially interested in me at this point and sat as close to my chair as possible. They were polite and attentive to crumbs or possible spillage. The main plate was pork sausage served with brown gravy and perfectly crispy, fried, sliced potatoes. The dogs continued their love affair with me, which I encouraged by slipping little morsels of sausage down to them. A selection of four cheeses followed, and the meal was finished with a chocolate mousse. The portions were generous without being wasteful. The meal for two people, including wine, cost 30 euros, or about $38.

A missing step in the normal restaurant experience was that no one took our meal order. It wasn't necessary. Madame Nicole, who had been a chef for over 60 years, decided what the menu would be each day. There were no printed menus to be found at the restaurant. There was one choice for each course, and they were all delicious and dog-approved.

"My mother taught me how to cook, " Chef told me. She was about to tell me more, but her young, 75-year-old friend came over.

"Oh, someone new is here. Where are you from?" he asked. Of course I told him California and he was thrilled. "I like California, and you have very nice calves. Are you an actress? I bet you play sports. No, wait, tell me, are you married?"

"Yes, I am," I managed to say, laughing.

"Well, point him out to me. I want to see if I could win in a fight."

"But monsieur, I came to France to learn French, not to find a man."

His septuagenarian friends were sitting around a table close by, and they enjoyed the whole exchange. They roared with laughter. They shouted encouragements to him but also insults like "As usual he failed," and they wished him better luck the next time.

"Eh, I'll be dead the next time a pretty woman from California comes here."

* * * * * * *

Another restaurant, located in an old, former one-room schoolhouse, was truly French as well, but entirely different in style. La Récréation (The Recess) revived the extremely rural, dying French hamlet of Les Arques. The American writer Michael S. Sanders took his family to Les Arques to live for a year in order to write about the evolution of the hamlet in his book, *From Here You Can't See Paris*. He described what life here was like before and after the opening of the restaurant, how it affected the community members, and what owning and operating a restaurant involved. I bought this book as soon as it was published in 2005 and loved it so much that I have re-read it many times. So it was not surprising or a burden for me to venture a mere

38 kilometers away for the noon meal at La Récréation. It was so thrilling to step into the setting of one of my favorite books. And it looked and smelled just like I hoped it would.

The large gravel schoolyard had colorful tablecloths on the numerous tables, which were filled with families and friends. Large trees shaded some parts of the yard. Flowers were blooming along the black metal border fence and in all the pots on the schoolhouse steps. The schoolhouse had white shutters on all the windows, and the roofline reminded me of Flemish buildings I had seen in Belgium with the facade "steps" along the top of the building. The schoolhouse had been divided into three rooms to accommodate the restaurant. There was the spotless white kitchen Mr Sanders had described so well, the dining room, and the brilliant red-walled entry room, which housed the bar as well. We were greeted by the co-owner and I felt like I knew her because of reading the book. I'd lived vicariously through their difficult opening years with so many hardships, and I knew of their successes too. For just meeting someone, I knew so much about her. She probably wondered why I had such a goofy smile on my face and kept saying, "I am so happy to be here." Or maybe she realized I was just another fan.

Sander's book explained how the business became a community-wide effort. For example, Chef created a trademark garnish for every plate – a stuffed squash blossom with goat cheese and herbs. Chef only wanted fresh French food, but being isolated was a problem. Community members understood the importance of the restaurant's success to the village and they saw how hard the couple worked. In a short time, neighbors donated fresh produce from their garden and successful hunters returning from a hunting trip would offer freshly butchered deer meat for that day's main plate.

When my plate was finally placed in front of me, and there was my stuffed squash blossom, I actually became teary-eyed. It meant so much to me to be a diner at this place I'd read so much about that my French almost disappeared. When I saw the blossom, I exclaimed, "Oh there it is. It is true." The waitress smiled and nodded knowingly.

"Yes, the book is true," she said.

* * * * * * *

I was making noticeable progress with my French, yet I still didn't know how solidly engrained it was. I never dreamed in French. I often translated almost word for word in my head and then adjusted the sentence before I said it out loud. And the challenge of understanding every single word still eluded me. Would my French be there for me in any kind of situation? If I witnessed an emergency or a crime, could I help? I just didn't know. The police might not have the patience for a witness with a dictionary. With enough advance notice, I could be prepared for anything, but the nagging question of my competency still lingered—until one rainy Saturday.

Even though it was summer, it was raining. Not uncommon this year. The summer crowds had arrived and were trying to make the most of their vacations. People rented canoes, went on picnics, and took walks along the marked trails. One of those marked trails happened to follow our narrow, steep driveway. To be honest, the driveway looked more like a walking trail than a lane for cars. Often, as I slowly inched up the lane in first gear, I had to wait for people to notice me, wait for them to accept that a car could actually fit, and wait for them to finally step out of the way. About halfway up the *petit rue*, climbing rose vines brushed the side of the car, and there were four houses that opened immediately onto the street, with the inhabitant's first step. When my car passed pedestrians, they had to squeeze flat along the wall, practically holding their stomachs in and turning their feet sideways. I endured this slow obstacle course because there was a small garage I could use opposite my rental house. The space was only big enough for one car, although it did house my small pile of firewood, and a damaged, wood canoe hanging from

the ceiling. As long as I drove halfway past the opening of the garage, then made a sharp, ninety-degree turn into the space, I was golden. Stone walls were nothing to fear.

On this particular Saturday, the rock wall won, and it had help. About halfway up the hill, I saw something that made my heart sink: there in the middle of the lane was a large group of elementary school children. A walking field trip to the Château at the top of my hill must have taken place during the early afternoon, and now the children were heading back down to the school. They were taking their sweet time, as only five year olds can do, enjoying the flowers, kicking stones, holding hands to whisper secrets, and calling to every cat they saw on the rock walls. It was a traffic jam of little people. The solitary teacher could have used a sheepdog. She herded the majority down the hill, then went back to gather the few strays out of the cats' courtyard, while at the same time ordering the few boys on the rock wall ledge to get down and away from the steep drop. She was doing an excellent job, and I admired her patience from the comfort of my air-conditioned car while I listened to soothing music. When it looked like the last of the little cuties had walked past, after rubbing designs in the dirty side of my car with their artistic fingers, I continued driving to the garage. I smiled to myself thinking, "There is no cuter sound than little children speaking French. They are so adorable. If I could take care of two perfectly behaved little French children, my French would improve by leaps and ..., WHAT IS THAT?"

A jarring sight interrupted not just my daydream of a perfect job, but also my perfect turn into the garage. I violently turned the wheel before even considering the consequence to the car, because I saw something. No, it was someone. Thank goodness it wasn't a child, but there immediately in front of the car's bumper in the middle of my garage was a seventy-year-old woman standing on a box. She wore knee-high white socks with sandals and a long, flowery, loose dress. Hanging around her neck was a long-lens expensive camera. She was standing on her tiptoes on the box to get a better view inside the canoe and, judging from the way her tongue was hanging out of the side of her mouth, her concentration was completely absorbed in the task. I saw her, then she saw me—causing her eyes to grow wide—and I heard a dreadful metallic tearing sound coming from the hindquarter of my car.

I slammed on the brakes to avoid further damage to the car and squeezed my eyes shut. English swear words came out of my mouth, and I jerked open the door.

"What are you doing? Why are you here?" I demanded. Even though my tone was angry, inside I was extremely pleased with myself for speaking in French.

"I am so sorry," she said.

"I hit the wall with my car."

"OH, I am so very sorry. You have an interesting canoe, and I was just trying to see it to take a picture of it. It has a kind of beauty."

"It is a shit old boat." Then I realized how awful it would have been if someone was hurt. " Well, it is better to hit my car than to hit you."

"I am sorry about your car."

"No, a person is more important than a car. It is all right."

She walked away slowly, with her head down, and I knew she felt terrible. Not terrible enough to offer to help pay for the damages but awful enough to feel guilty. It was too bad the accident had to happen, but it was a small price to pay to learn that my French could be relied upon even in an emergency situation.

Je Ne Toi Oublierai Jamais

(I Will Never Forget You)

It was Friday, one of my favorite days of the week, because the local newspaper was published that day. I walked to my favorite store, The Press, with my French dictionary in hand to buy the newspaper. I was already mentally planning what to drink at the café while I read the paper, and I was hoping that there would be a full week of social activities and events in the articles. A stack of about thirty newspapers could always be found on the counter between the cash register and the national lottery cards.

The area around the cash register was the most important place in the whole store: it was the communication hub. The amount of local news shared by word of mouth far outweighed the amount of news in the newspaper. Maybe the oral news was not fit to be printed nor validated by fact checkers, but it was always interesting. When it was my turn to be helped at the counter, there still were five or six locals milling around the counter, just visiting with each other. My correct, exact change, using the pesky, one and two cent coins, was all ready in my fist, and I nonchalantly reached for the newspaper. The space was completely empty. I looked at the locals' hands. No one was holding a paper. Was there a run on the paper? Was there something big going on that I didn't know about?

"Are there no more newspapers?" I asked.

"Oh, they are closed for two weeks for their vacation," Madame told me.

"The newspaper closed? What about what's happening? How will I know?"

People all around me were shaking their heads and shrugging their shoulders. One man told me, "Well, we just know. It's the same routine every year."

"They want their vacations like everyone. It is a stressful job," someone else said.

My eyes were still wide with astonishment, and I must have had an "I lost my puppy" look, because Madame gave me a comforting smile and rubbed my upper arm. I didn't want to come off as an ugly American, but I ventured a suggestion. "Well, maybe one person goes on vacation (the past tense of "can" was still too difficult for me), but we have our newspaper. Then another person goes on vacation the second week, when the first person is back in the office, and we have our newspaper that week too," I offered as a radical idea.

Everybody started talking at once. The good news was that everyone understood my French; the bad news was that they disagreed with me.

"No, that wouldn't work..."

"It is an easy job..."

"My sister works at the newspaper, and she said..."

"Americans don't have vacation time like we do, so..."

I couldn't follow the conversation, because everyone was talking at the same time. In a matter of seconds, it became a lengthy, loud debate. More locals came into the store, bought what they needed, and then joined in the debate. Madame conducted business while enjoying the show.

Weeks later, I had another encounter involving the newspaper. I had an appointment with the newspaper editor to review the short thank-you article I had written in French. I wanted to publicly thank the kind people of Cénac et St. Julien and Domme for their warm welcome throughout my stay. The bald, elderly editor, complete with bow tie, invited me to sit before his desk while he diplomatically refined my note. He kept adjusting his reading glasses up and down the bridge of his nose, like he couldn't believe the words on the page. Still, there wasn't too much red ink needed due to errors. His suggestions made my note more precise, while still retaining my voice. Then all of a sudden, he stopped reading and slowly raised his head to look questioningly at me.

"I don't believe you meant to say this last sentence," he said. He turned the page to face me and placed his little finger on the sentence in question. I re-read my French sentence, and in my mind I knew I had written "You all have a special place in my heart." A little corny, but I meant it in the nicest way.

The editor continued, "I wrote that this experience will always hold special remembrance for you. You see, your sentence is a term of endearment that one says to someone that one loves. You do not love everyone in Cénac et St. Julien, do you?" He had a slight smile while politely waiting for my answer.

"Oh, no, I did not mean to say that," I said.

He nodded and continued with his red pen, "French is the language of love, so one must be careful."

On the day my announcement was published, I had a hair appointment in Cénac et St. Julien. The hair salon was a great place to practice French, and the owner Natalie was one of those people who made you feel like an old friend. From my very first appointment, I had told her that she would be my French teacher who had chemicals. She had laughed and said she would do her best to help me. Now during this particular visit many months later, I used all six verb tenses that I knew (past, present, future, conditional, subjunctive, and imperfect), plus I understood most of the complex conversation whirling around the salon. An American customer with very limited French came in, and I translated for her. Afterwards, I couldn't believe I was able to do it, and I mentioned my wonder to Natalie, who was cutting my hair.

"You have great courage to learn French. I admire you. It is a difficult language, and everyone knows it is more difficult when a person is older," she said.

"I just hope I don't forget everything when I am back in California."

"Oh Karen, that is easy to avoid. Just come back."

The conversation turned to my announcement in the day's newspaper and my silly error. Natalie laughed and made sure the others in the shop heard about my adventure in the editor's office. After repeating my error, she exclaimed, "Oh that editor! He should have left your words alone. It would have been charming."

* * * * * * *

So did I become fluent in French? Fluent enough to understand every word said in a conversation and every word spoken on the radio? No, I didn't. The amount of knowledge I gained was impressive considering that when I arrived I could only speak in the present and past tense. Based on my knowledge of verb tense, there was no future. Luckily it only took a couple of months of being in Cénac et St. Julien for a 'future' to became part of my speech. Over time I added the conditional, the imperfect, the subjunctive, and the other past tenses. I remembered almost a year before as I boarded my plane for France, I narrowly set my goal to be able to speak, dream, gossip, and swear in French. I achieved three out of four of my goals, with dreaming being the missing skill. Although swearing in French became my secret skill since I never used it.

I was so focused on language that I wasn't conscious of the human element of this pursuit, either to me or to others. Habitually risking rejection by speaking to strangers especially in a new language placed me in a vulnerable spot. I learned to be comfortable with making mistakes and asking for help. For a person like me who likes to be in control, that was a big change. I learned to trust people at least until they proved my trust misplaced, but that never happened. I learned to let down my guard and in the process I became more interested in people. Chance encounters, hearing about a stranger's life was enjoyable. I especially liked visiting with older people. Thanks to French, I became more curious and trusting of people. Gradually over time my quest had widened beyond verb tenses and slang knowledge, as friendships became more important, and my place in the community was formed. My desire morphed into wanting to learn about my friends in my new home. Language lessons moved off a dated schoolbook page and on to a real person standing in front of me. Lessons truly were all around me, happening any time of the day, at any place. There was always more knowledge, and I had lots more to learn. I knew where I would go to refresh my French. I knew where I would go to touch my heart again.

My last day in my adopted French home consisted of twelve tight, long hugs, ten answers to 'when will you come back?', four small bon voyage parties, three bottles of champagne, two super generous, sincere invitations of lodging if I return needing a place to stay, and one sweet last French class. Miracle of miracles, there were zero tears from me, although there were many times I had to take slow deep breaths.

"I can't believe that you're leaving already," Hazel said.

"It went by too fast, yet it's like you've always been here," Sue added.

"I will never forget you. On class days when I'm back in California, I'll think of you guys in this attic working away," I said.

"Give me a hug, love. Fuck, I think I'm going to cry," Emma said.

After class I had more good-byes that needed to be said, so I slowly dragged my feet down the hill trying to put them off. It was a sad day, and it was going to become sadder. The lights were on in Claire's kitchen. I knew Claire and Henri wouldn't mind if I dropped in.

"Claire and Henri, you two are good friends, and I can not thank you enough for all that you did for me."

 "It was a joy to have you as a neighbor and as a friend. Now when I look at that house, I will think of you," Claire said.

"And when we hear California on the television, we will think of you too," Henri said.

"Well, if it is something really crazy about California, then do not think of me."

"No, only good things. You are only associated with good things," they said.

Gâteau Noix Colette (Colette's Walnut Cake)

3 *oeufs* (3 eggs)

1 *verre sucre* (1 cup sugar)

1 *verre de farine* (1 cup flour)

1 *sachet levure* (1 packet of baking powder)

2 *verres de noix broyees* (2 cups of finely chopped walnuts)

½ *verre d'huile* (1/2 cup oil)

1 *pincee de sel* (1 pinch salt)

1 *verre de crème fraiche* (1 cup of sour cream, or crème fraiche if you can find it)

 Faites cuire au four 220 C (Bake at 220 degrees)

All year I ate a variety of walnut cakes because my area was known for its walnuts. There were other walnut products too like mustard, oil, and candies; however, the walnut cake seemed to be the item that appeared on every restaurant menu and at every social function. Later on after visiting with Claire and Henri, I sat down with Jean-Paul and Colette on their flower-filled terrace to say our good-byes. We exchanged addresses and promised to keep in touch. While we were visiting, Colette brought out her homemade, chocolate-frosted walnut cake (the best walnut cake I had the whole year), and on her second trip she had the fancy drinking glasses and champagne.

"I will always remember the truffles," I said.

"It was nothing. I wish you could have seen the dog work. He is a genius."

"Well, he understands French better than me."

"No, no. He understands French better than my son-in-law."

Acknowledgements

My first thanks must go to the people of Cénac et St. Julien and Domme. Without their patience and friendship, my stay would have been a quiet, lonely one and this book would not have been possible. My heartfelt thanks to Heidi Mitchell and Jill Benitz, my very thorough editors, who helped me so much. It was a pleasure to have them on my side. All the remaining grammatical violations are all mine. Finally my love and thanks to my husband, Steve, who was my biggest supporter in writing this book and in life.

Made in the USA
San Bernardino, CA
10 July 2016